The Undressed Manager

About the Author

Jim Myers started out in this 'development' business as a Peace Corps Volunteer in 1965. He was assigned to a small village in Andhra Pradesh, India with the instructions to teach local farmers the new deep litter system of poultry rearing. A noble gesture....which also became his first experience as 'the undressed manager.' Since 1965 Jim has lived and worked in more than 40 developing countries in Asia, Africa, The Balkans and former Soviet Union countries. He has worked for the UN, international NGOs and the private sector on a wide range of projects funded by western donors and governments. He has during his more then 42 years seen so many well meaning, dedicated people fall flat on their backside because they were NOT given the 'basic tools' for managing and implementing projects. He now hopes to rectify this problem for the future development programme professionals through his handbook 'The Undressed Manager'. Read it .....and then do it better!

What

'The Barefoot Doctor'

was to

Health Care Providers,

'THE UNDRESSED MANAGER'

is to

development programmes and project personnel

Jim Myers

Readworthy

New Delhi

First published 2009

Readworthy Publications (P) Ltd.

Regd. Off.: A-18, Mohan Garden
Near Nawada Metro Station
New Delhi – 110 059 (India)
Phone: 011-2537 1324
Fax: +91-11-2537 1323

Branch: 4662/21, Ansari Road
Daryaganj
New Delhi – 110 002
Phone: 011-43549197
Fax: +91-11-23243060

Email: info@readworthypub.com

Web: www.readworthypub.com

ISBN 13: 978-81-89973-74-2 ISBN 10: 81-89973-74-6

Printed at Salasar Imaging Systems, Delhi - 35

Dedication and Thanks

I would like to dedicate this book to my grandson-Jaik Stephen Wolfe, who is only six months old, but already shows signs of being a good project manager. Also, to his mommy, my daughter Pia Myers, who grew up in several Asian and African countries...and who I hope will someday return to do humanitarian work in the developing world. And to my son-in-law Brian, who will hopefully continue being a good 'manager' of his wonderful family.

I asked three close friends, all of whom have dedicated their lives to work in the developing world, to review this book for content and usefulness. Without any hesitation they all agreed and spent endless hours making sure I got things right. My warm and sincere thanks to Mr. Louis Kuhn, a kind and caring individual and excellent trainer, who is now retired from the Foreign Service; Mr. Ron Burkard, mentor, guide, leader, and an extremely capable manager, and my former boss in CARE; Dr. David Calder, the medical profession's loss, but a real gain to the developing world's health programmes because of his wit and wisdom...now if he could only learn how to play golf!

Foreword

More often then not organizations send their well meaning people out to some developing countries with little more than a handful of money and some encouraging words. Their orders are…establish an office, start a new programme and call me when you have 'things' set-up.

This handbook has been prepared to better describe those 'THINGS' that are to be set up… And to provide some support and guidance to the energetic, but perhaps inexperienced, new 'Project Manager.' It is the author's desire that this book becomes as useful to managers and project personnel as the book 'The Barefoot Doctor' is to the under-equipped and less skilled medical personnel working in remote areas of the world.

The handbook includes:

- Definition of terms… To keep you up to date and straight on today's 'development set' jargon (which by the way will need to be updated regularly).
- Checklists… Covering the mundane, but essential administrative tasks, including legal issues on forming an organization.
- Examples of proposals… What goes into a technical proposal, with a special focus on how to raise project funds.
- Illustrations…of ToRs, MoUs, Log Frames, Corporate Capability Statements, Business plans and;
- 101 Management Tips… complete with exercises…. to strengthen your programme management skills.

Disclaimer: The Undressed Manager is a handbook of established and universally accepted international management tools and practices. These tools and concepts have been published separately by other authors, organizations and/or institutions. What the author of this book has done is to compile these various concepts/techniques, obtained from a variety of sources and based on 40 years of practical experience adapted them for use by "a first time programme manager." The adaptation takes into consideration... The reader's mother tongue is often not English and that many lay persons are involved in programme management, and have no formal academic training in management. The author acknowledges that most of the concepts and techniques described in this handbook are from other sources, and he lays no claim to being the originator. In case any copyrighted material has not been acknowledged please do write to the author/publisher for necessary amendments in the subsequent editions. When and where the original source of the material is known by the author, appropriate credit and acknowledgement is given. Any person requesting the specific source of a concept/technique not already identified should write to the author in care of the publisher, and attempts will be made to identify the original source. Management is not an exact science, there are no right or wrong answers and every person has his/her own view on the subject.

Contents

Annexes

Introduction

The Intent

In this publication I have taken great steps... And searched the depths of my ever deteriorating mind...to ensure this manual was practical and useful to anybody currently involved with humanitarian development programmes and/or for those who plan to be involved in project management in the future.

If this book seems to be personal in nature and biased towards what I believe is correct... Well, that's because it was designed that way. If you want to look at sophisticated processes, models and methods, may I suggest you visit some of the management websites on the internet. In this handbook, I've tried to show you how it works in reality. And because it's not a perfect world – therefore this is not a perfect handbook...but I hope a good read none the less.

This handbook does provide a great deal of 'food for thought' on how to design and implement programmes and will, hopefully serve as a basic reference guide with tips and suggestions that can be used by all development programme personnel (please see 'how to use this handbook' in the following section).

Some of the resource materials covered and presented in this handbook may already be well understood by some; for others the materials may be new and more useful. Many of the concepts are older, and more basic, and have been taken from materials produced by the UN, NGOs and professional trainers. In writing this handbook I was however, surprised at how 'little' things have actually changed in forty years.

I do hope this handbook includes something for everybody to use and apply in their projects. You may use this handbook as a field reference and support guide...or however, it best suits your needs and the professional growth of your staff.

The handbook was designed primarily for mid or junior level management staff who are, or will be, involved with the setting up, organizing, running and management of organizations...and managing Development Projects. The text of this handbook has focused on planning and implementation of humanitarian development programmes, that can be initiated in the developing countries of Asia, Africa, the Balkans and the CIS/CEE region. The contents of the handbook will hopefully eliminate the need for too much 'home office' support... which the author always found to be a pain in the backside anyway.

Topics introduced in this handbook include a wide range of universally accepted design, planning, implementation and management concepts which have been adopted for more practical application from a number of published works written by too many other authors to mention. In addition, many of the ideas, tips and tools on how to structure new programmes suitable for donor funding have been adopted from donor's publications and once again adopted for practical use. And without 'dreaming' too much...the author hopes the suggestions provided herein will hopefully lead to more effective, efficient and sustainable programmes in the future...I know your donors are hoping for the same thing too.

How to use this handbook?

This handbook has been divided into three chapters.

Chapter I takes a look at the various management styles and covers leadership traits useful in programme and project management and implementation. This chapter also includes management 'Tips' that will refresh your own management skills and, with some slight revisions, can be used as the basis for in-house management training courses for team building.

Chapter II reviews the steps necessary to open a new office and get a new programme up and running. A solid beginning usually means less headaches and problems later on. Particular attention should be paid to legal registration... An increasingly more difficult issue from both the donor and host government side.

Chapter III gets into the 'nitty-gritty' of programme management and implementation...including results based management plus materials on how to make your programme more sustainable...which is on everybody's mind these days... Also covers a broader area of marketing, management and finance.

The 'how to' information contained in this handbook is presented in various ways:

- Checklists: To serve as a reminder of what is needed
- Step by step procedures: For improving efficiency
- Examples of different development approaches and;
- Modern management tools: For effective programming

In addition, samples of various planning and financial models, plus examples of work plans, ToRs and other management support tools, such as log frames and manning charts can be found in the Annex of this handbook.

Abbreviations and Acronyms

CBD	Community Based Development
ECD	Early Childhood Development
FGD	Focus Group Discussion
GONGO	Governmental non-government organization
HR	Human Resources
ICR	Indirect Cost Recovery
IT	Information Technology
MBO	Management by Objectives
MDG	Millennium Development Goals
M&E	Monitoring and Evaluation
MIS	Management Information Systems
MoU	Memorandum of Understanding
NGO	Non-Governmental Organization
PR	Public Relations
PRA	Participatory Research Action
PRSP	Poverty Reduction Strategy Programme
RBM	Results Based Management
SWAP	Sector Wide Approach Programme
SWOT	Strengths, Weakness, Opportunities, Threats
TA	Technical Assistance
ToR	Terms of Reference
UN	United Nations
UNICEF	United Nations Children's Fund

Glossary of Terms

- **Action Plans**...are a refinement of the overall work plan/approach and developed after the original work plan has been approved; action plans take the work plans one step further by better defining what needs to be accomplished and set the stage for project implementation; action plans are based on the work plans submitted in the original technical proposal and usually cover one year of activities.
- **Administration Costs...** General operation costs (rent, utilities) for running an organization; these costs are usually non-project specific and can include regional/country costs.
- **Advocacy**... To advocate, promote, lobby a concept and/or belief in an effort to sway opinions of decision makers...to speak out on or for a specific topic (example: ECD as a project intervention).
- **Award contract**... A legal document signing/giving a contract to an organization for writing a winning technical proposal on a specified project/or amount of work; contains obligations and tasks, including funding levels, to be completed by the organization.
- **Benchmarks/Baseline**... The starting/beginning point; the situation as it exists before the implementation of a project begins (example: 'X' % of villagers do not have safe drinking water); baselines can also be the basis for an evaluation and often determined by a Situation Analysis or needs assessment survey.
- **Beneficiaries**... The people/groups of people who receive direct benefits of the project activities; beneficiaries are usually part of the target groups; also known as rights holders.
- **Best Practices**... Internationally accepted set of standards for services; a Manager will use the set of best practices as a guide for establishing the norms in service provision and for efficient delivery of services.

- **Budget Control**... The monitoring of all financial expenditures/payments/receipts of funds... Usually by line item expenditures...includes project and non-project specific costs for personnel, operations, equipment; budget control is often based on financial forecasts or projections.
- **Budget Forecasting**... A financial planning exercise of projecting/estimating the required amount of money necessary to implement the projects and/or operate the organization for a specific time period; often decided (forecast) on a quarterly basis; Managers use budget forecasts for monitoring expenditures and requesting funds from the donor or main headquarters office.
- **Budget Line**... The individual expenditure heading (line item) of a project cost generally placed under broader headings...(example: Under the financial heading of project personnel...the budget lines would be (a) Project Manager, (b) Deputy Project Manager (c) Driver, etc.)
- **Budget Report**... The specific, detailed and timely reporting of all costs and financial expenditures, including inventory and equipment... Often broken down by project and non-project expenditures...as required in the contract award or memorandum of understanding (MoU).
- **Capacity**... The ability within a person/group/community/organization to achieve/undertake a specified task; ability (capacity) can be measured in both physical and/or intellectual terms.
- **Client-centred Approach**... Clients can be beneficiaries and/or part of the target group... The client-centred approach aims/provides/focuses project inputs/ services directly to the needs of the client.
- **Concept Paper**... A brief (3-4 page), detailed description of an idea/concept to be given to potential donors; concept papers introduce an idea for a new project or offer an improved approach/technique in an existing project; a concept paper should include goals/objectives, possible barriers, estimated costs and expected results.

- **Consortium**... A mix of donors and/or partners working together in unison on the same development effort...with each partner usually bringing separate/specific expertise to the development (consortium) approach.
- **Contingency Planning**... A back-up plan (second option) in case the original concept/approach fails; contingency plans include technical approaches as well as financial reserves.
- **Contractual Negotiations**... The art of 'discussing' relevant terms and conditions of an activity/specified amount of work in an effort to reach a mutually agreed upon statement, detailing the responsibilities of all parties involved; this document/statement will form the basis of a legally binding contract.
- **Cost Allocation**... The assigning of a specific amount of money to accomplish a defined task/activity... Often within a set time period; usually cost allocations are estimates, generally included in the budget forecasts and monitored under budget control.
- **Cost Justification**...A rational explanation, with complete documentation, of how, why and on whom the funds were spent and/or are planned to be spent questions on 'justifying' the costs can be asked by auditors/Managers and include: Why are the costs higher than planned/forecast...? Why was 'X' vendor paid this amount of money...? Did the expenditure produce the desired benefit/result/impact.
- **Donor**... person/organization who is providing the funding and/or other resources (equipment/personnel) in part or whole for programme operations or the undertaking of project activities.
- **Effectiveness**... Ability to accomplish set tasks/activities (output) and to reach the goals using the available resources; effectiveness is what is achieved rather than what one does.
- **Efficiency**... Ability to accomplish set tasks/activities in a timely, well coordinated manner; efficiency is the ratio of output to input and often equated to lower costs.

- **Evaluation**...is a process which attempts to determine as systematically and objectively as possible the relevance, effectiveness, efficiency and impact of the activities in light of specified objectives.
- **Expenditure**... An amount of money/time or other resource used (given) to undertake a task/activity.
- **Expertise**... The technical competence of an individual/group; expertise is usually asked for in an effort to supplement the organizational goals (when there is a gap in local know-how) and to more efficiently achieve results.
- **Financial Audits**... Routine inspection...from both internal and external auditors...of an organization's financial books/documents and covers both operations/ inventory and projects; items covered in an audit include: Funds received, payments made, inventory lists, equipment purchases, compliance to national tax regulations, bank details and procedures followed, financial record keeping systems established, financial checks and controls in place, supervision by management, reporting systems to donors/main office, tendering/ bidding procedures, and procurement guidelines/systems set-up among others.
- **Financial Management**... The art of planning and controlling the monetary aspects of the organization; good financial management usually means staying within the proposed/allocated budget, and demonstrating effective use of the available financial resources; financial management includes development of financial systems (budget forecasting, budget controls, reporting) for good cash flow and compliance to established financial rules and regulations established by the organization/donor/ local government authorities.
- **Fund-raising**... The art of attracting financial and/or other resources (equipment/personnel) needed from individuals or groups of potential donors who are willing to support...in cash or kind...the programme and project activities.
- **Grants**...differs from a loan in that it does not have to be paid back... Grants are a limited source of funding... often available

in cash or in kind... from other donor organizations/ individuals who are willing to support project activities; grants rarely cover operation or organization costs; to obtain a grant normally requires a detailed, written explanation on how the 'grant' funding will be used, on what activities, for how long and what are the expected results from the grant resources.

- **Harassment**... Cruel abuse, usually verbal but sometimes physical, that stems out of ignorance and disrespect of others; can be associated with gender, religion, capabilities or ethnic background.
- **Indirect Cost Recovery**... A mechanism that allows an implementing organization to recover costs associated with the running of an organization that cannot be directly linked and billed to a specific project.
- **Impact**... A measurable outcome or change as a result of an input or intervention; [example: Immunizations (input/outcome) reduce the risk of measles and benefits (impacts) on the child's overall health status].
- **Indicators**... are 'signs' (markers) that generally measure situations, impact or performance: A low level of literacy can be a sign (indicator) that kids don't go to school or that there are no proper schools/teachers available... An increase in a child's body weight can be a sign (indicator) of the impact of proper nutrition... Community health workers covering more/larger populations can be a sign (indicator) of performance as a result of better training/ equipment.
- **Input**...that which is produced/offered or given; (Please see outcomes/outputs below).
- **Institutionalise**... The placement of children/ adolescents in a common facility, either forced or voluntarily, who are removed from their family structure, but supervised by trained care-givers.
- **Integrate**... The weaving together (combining) of various and different components, skills and/or people to compliment and supplement the overall activity: ECD is a good example of

integrating the components of education and health/nutrition into one development approach.

- **Job Description**... A document presented to a new employee at the time of joining the organization that describes the terms, conditions, duties and responsibilities agreed between the employee and employer.
- **Leveraging**... The combining of resources, usually financial, that is used to extend the overall project services/components or give added value to an ongoing project providing for expansion or wider project coverage.
- **Log Frame**... A logical, step by step process that requires project planners/Managers to identify and rationalize the project objectives, activities, barriers and means to verify the expected results of projects during the project planning period; log frames are developed prior to project implementation and used for project monitoring.
- **M & E**...Monitoring and Evaluation...management tools for measuring project activities, progress and achievements.
- **Management By Objectives (MBO)**... A development-like (as opposed to a business-like) management process that focuses more on setting goals and achieving project objectives rather than on achieving actual results or creating change.
- **MDG**... Millennium Development Goals...global development targets set by the UN (see annex for list of MDGs).
- **Merger**... The bringing together/joining of two or more different entities/organizations for a common effort; merging of an organization/resources can strengthen sustainability efforts.
- **Mission Statement**... An organization's official and open statement which defines its purpose and mandate along with its development goals and objectives.
- **Monitoring**...is the periodic oversight of the implementation of an activity to establish or determine if the actions (work schedules, input deliveries) are proceeding according to plan.

- **Monitoring System**... A management process that uses previously defined indicators to measure the impact and/or performance of the project activities.
- **MOU**...Memorandum of Understanding... An official, legal agreement spelling out the terms and conditions between the project implementing partners, including host country governments.
- **Multiplier Effects**...when a single intervention provides multiple results or more than one benefit to the target group; (example: Improved child nutrition can also increase the chances of the child's learning ability because she/he is well enough to attend school on a more regular basis).
- **Narrative Reporting**... A brief, spoken/written presentation of the project activities/results usually given to donors.
- **Needs Assessment**... Usually a study, survey or research activity that determines the current situation (felt needs) in the designated project area; the findings from a Needs Assessment can be used to serve as the basis for a concept paper or technical proposal...or as the first step in the implementation of a new project; Needs Assessment can also establish benchmarks for future evaluations or new project activities.
- **Nepotism**...Usually the result of 'favouring' a close friend, relative or employee and providing that person with extra benefits and/or opportunities not given to everyone on an equal basis.
- **Non-Verbal Communication**... Communicating to others without the use of spoken words or written text... A hand gesture, facial expression or a wink of the eye can be considered non-verbal communication; certain behaviours can be 'non-verbal' communication.
- **Office Management**... The running/supervision of the administrative and personnel office functions that provide support to the organization/projects.

- **Operation Costs...** The direct, non-project financial expenditures incurred in the management and support services of an organization.
- **Organization**...is the registered legal entity under which the organization operates in country, receives donor funds, and conducts programme/project activities.
- **Organisational Policy**...is an organizational statement, usually based and prepared on a proven strategy, that dictates the common decisions and/or rules and regulations of an organization; policies can be applied to personnel (example: Number of leave days granted in a year) to project activities, on vehicle use (example: Private versus official) and on organizational direction (example: The policy of this organization is to work with only the poorer communities).
- **Organisational Strategy**... An organizational strategy is developed as part of a unified plan that ties all parts of the organization together; an organizational strategy forges the organization's goals/objectives and helps to formulate the policy.
- **Outcomes**...is the impact of the intervention/activity on the target (group) audience; outcomes are monitored by indicators; (example of both outcomes and outputs: You conduct a training course,...the inputs are the training materials/modules produced for the course...the outputs are more people trained/given new knowledge... The outcomes are the impact (change/improvement) on the target group because of what the newly trained people actually did with their new training knowledge.
- **Outputs**...that which is learned/produced, but does not necessarily have an impact on the intended audience (target group).
- **Overheads**... Administrative expenditures like office rent, utilities and programme support staff that are related to programme operations but that cannot be billed/charged directly to a specific project.

- **Participatory Approach...** Joint involvement of beneficiaries, partners, stakeholders and counterparts in project activities include planning, decision making and training; any activity seeking the involvement and participation of others.
- **Performance Appraisal**... Assessment of a staff/team member's job performance; other terms, besides Performance Appraisal, used to describe the evaluation of an employee's job performance include - Annual Employee Evaluation and Performance Review; the evaluation of an employee's job performance should be conducted at least once a year by the employee's supervisor and is based on his/her ability to carryout the tasks/duties described in his/her Job Description.
- **Phase out**... The gradual reduction of the organization's involvement and/or contribution to a specific activity/project, which eventually leads to the closing down and 'handing over' of specified activities/projects or programme operations.
- **Problem Statement**... A detailed description of the existing/felt needs of the target group; a basis for implementing project activities; Problem Statements are included in concept papers/technical proposals and are the basis for any action/interventions taken; (example: The 'problem' can be...high infant mortality, lack of safe drinking water, etc.)
- **Programme**... For the purposes of this handbook the term 'programme' will be used to define both the organization, as an entity, as well as combined group of projects being implemented under the entity/organization's authority.
- **Programme Management**... The art of leading, supervising and managing a group of qualified people, including the effective use of available resources (vehicles, office equipment, finances) for conducting various specified activities as mandated and prescribed by the organization.
- **Programme Manager**... The person responsible for the overall organization and effective programme management and execution of project plans and activities (see above-programme management) that includes personnel, finances, vehicles/

equipments, reporting, fund raising, donor, government and organization liaison and operations.

- **Project**... A detailed activity/intervention consisting of one or more components necessary to achieve the identified project goal/objectives.
- **Project Coordinator**... A person responsible for the support and liaison of an ongoing project between direct project staff and the organization's administration support... This person is **not** involved in the implementation or management of the daily project activities.
- **Project Costs**... An allocation of funds/resources that are direct expenditures related to the planning/execution of the project activity and which are necessary for the implementation, management, monitoring and evaluation of the project activity; project costs do **not** generally include administrative or general programme (overhead) expenditures.
- **Project Field Staff**... A team member assigned to undertake project duties in the district/village (field) and who regularly work outside the head quarter's office.
- **Project Manager**... A person directly responsible for the **overall** efficient and effective implementation of a specified project activity/activities as detailed in the project proposal; Project Managers generally report to the Programme Managers.
- **Project Methodology**... The approach or strategy adopted for implementing the project activities; Methodologies explain the way the project will be implemented; (example: CBD is a methodology).
- **Project Officer**... A person directly responsible for the efficient and effective implementation of a specific project activity as detailed in the project proposal; usually reports to Project Coordinator or Project Manager.
- **Project Proposal**... The document that describes in detail, usually including the financial costs, the complete information on how the project will be implemented and managed including: Background (historical as well as technical), Problem

Statement (needs), Goals and Objectives, Methodology (approach), Implementation Steps, Personnel Requirements, time frame for Implementation, Strategy and Log Frame.

- **Project Sustainability**... Providing a means/basis for continuing the project activity after the initial funding and external development assistance has been withdrawn/phased out; Project Sustainability can be in the terms of Management, Financial and Technical Sustainability.
- **PRSP**... Poverty Reduction Strategy Programme: Paper prepared by Governments and The World Bank that describes a country's macroeconomic structural and social policies and define programmes that are designed to promote growth and reduce poverty.
- **Public Relations (PR)**... For the purposes of this handbook Public Relations (PR) will be defined as the promotion of the organization's attributes and capacities meant for enhancement to the image of the organization.
- **RBM**... Results Based Management... Project Implementation that produces evidence (results) of achievement rather than goal accomplishment.
- **Risk Management**... A style of management that involves choosing between possible alternatives that can have an element of 'risk' during the implementation phase of a project activity.
- **Scale up**... The phased strengthening or up grading of project services...not necessarily an expansion; (example: A community can be initially provided with hand pumps for safe drinking, which can later be 'scaled–up' to include household connections).
- **Seed Grants**... Usually a relatively small sum of money made available for introducing a new project concept/approach or idea... Seed Money is meant to 'plant' an idea or show potential results in an effort to entice other donors/communities to accept the new idea and to provide additional resources for expanding this new activity.

- **Seed Money**... Funds generated from ongoing activities undertaken during the implementation of the project that can be used for increasing activities or expansion; (example: Funds generated from the sale of handicrafts can be Seed Money for purchasing new project sewing machines).
- **Situational Analysis**... A Situational Analysis is the thorough review of data, information and circumstances made after the scientific collection (using surveys/research) of relevant statistics of a specified community/target group; the findings will be applied to the Project Design to ensure more effective results; Situation Analysis is sometimes inter-changeable with the term 'Needs Assessment'.
- **Sponsors**...are individuals/companies that contribute, in cash or kind, to specific components of your organization/project and who expect to have recognition of 'their' contribution displayed and/or acknowledged; sponsors differ from donors in several ways: (1) The contribution is generally very specific in nature, (2) Sponsorships are smaller in value and; (3) Usually a 'one-off' contribution.
- **Stakeholders**... Those individuals or communities who play an active role in the project; who are part of the decision making process and have made an investment in the project... And who often stand to benefit directly or indirectly from the project's interventions; also known as duty bearers.
- **Supervision**... More closely related to coordination because of the 'overseeing' of activities or specific tasks; supervision is the guidance and direction often provided by an employee's immediate 'boss,' supervision is not the daily or overall management of the tasks and activities.
- **SWAP**...Sector Wide Approach Programme...is a World Bank motivated concept included in most sector development reforms (health, education, etc.)... Main purpose is to eliminate vertical programmes, reduce donor duplication and to give the governments more financial control and ownership.
- **SWOT**...Strengths, Weakness, Opportunities, Threats... A form of analysis when determining a Project Design or Methodology

(approach); SWOT findings can help in the preparation of business plans or the re-assessment of a programme or an organization.

- **Target Group**... The beneficiaries of the intended project activities; a segment of the community or population (example: Youth), who will be the main focus of the project intervention.
- **Technical Assistance (TA)**... The use of specialized skills/training/expertise to compliment planned/ ongoing project activities; TA is usually provided by consultants.
- **Time Management**... The art of managing time more efficiently for better productivity through good time usage (prioritizing, planning) and by reducing 'time wasters'.
- **ToR**...Terms of Reference... A document that spells out the requirements, needs and specific conditions for a certain task/project activity; ToRs can be developed for individual consultant's tasks, partners or for Project Implementation.
- **UN**...United Nations.
- **UNICEF**...United Nations Children's Fund.
- **Verbal Communication**... The art of communicating and conveying the message(s) clearly through the spoken word (communication)...includes both, one-way and two-way communication.
- **Vertical Programme**... A project activity that stands alone/isolated and independently operated; vertical programmes are not integrated into the mainstream of the government's national plan/programme; nor is the project cross sectorial in design.
- **Visibility**... For the purposes of this handbook the term 'visibility' will describe a media method used to promote both the organization and the organization's programmes/projects to the general public.
- **Vision**... The forward, and often creative, thinking (into the future) by the Manager/Director who can detail needs, strategies and see the end results of a project activity; vision provides future direction of a programme or organization.

- **Work Plan**... A document that details **all** components/activities/steps necessary to implement a project activity, including allocation of costs and utilization of resources; Work Plans are usually integrated into National Work Plans, require approval and follow the approach/schedules described in the Technical Proposal.
- **Written Communication**... The art of communicating and conveying the message/instruction/plan clearly through the written word (communication); (examples: Written Instructions, Internal Memos, E-Mails, Brochures, Pamphlets, Posters and Project Report).

Note: The source for many of these terms comes from a guide to project development written for CCF by the same author

Vision, Decision
and
Supervision

1 Management and Leadership

1.1 The Art of Management

So you've been hired or perhaps even promoted to the position of 'Manager'... Congratulations and good luck to you in your new position!

In developing countries, and even in some international organizations, the term Manager is often used to describe a Supervisor, Administrator, Project Officer, and Director. Whatever you are being called please be sure you and your immediate boss...or the person who does your performance appraisal...are in agreement when it comes to **'what are your tasks and what are you actually responsible for achieving.'**

Regardless of the title, programme management makes you responsible for:

- ☑ **Providing Programme Vision**
- ☑ **Making Programme and Financial Decisions**
- ☑ **The Overall Supervision**

...please try to
remember
these 3 points

You will develop the 'art of management' over time, and it will help if you remember:

MANAGEMENT
• Is an ongoing process. • Usually changes from job to job. • Everyone has a management style.

You can find out what your management style is by taking one of the many diagnostic tests. And it's always fun to see if these tests indicate the type of Manager **you think or believe you are**. You would be surprised to learn how many people feel they manage in one style and end up after taking the test, actually demonstrating a totally different style of management. The next section covers different management styles.

1.2 Management Styles

All Managers have a unique style of management (leaders also have a leadership style). Generally, these styles fall into a variation of eight different models of management behaviour. These eight styles combine **task orientation, relationship orientation, and effectiveness.** Different books have different definitions of the styles and terms...Here is my version.

Task Orientation: The extent to which a Manager directs his/her staff's efforts, towards **goal attainment**...and is characterized by planning, organization and controlling.

Relationship Orientation: Refers to what extent a Manager has **personal job relationships**, which are characterized by mutual trust, respect for staff ideas and consideration of feelings of others.

Effectiveness: The extent to which a Manager **achieves output** as required by his/her position.

Descriptions of eight management styles are given below. Often there is one dominant style of management, which is accompanied by a supporting management style. Management styles usually change when the person's position, or title; environment and job responsibilities change.

Descriptions of eight management styles
1. **Executive**: Uses a high task and relationship orientation. Executives are seen as good motivators who set high standards and prefer team management.
2. **Compromiser**: Uses a high task and relationship orientation in a situation that requires a high orientation to only one or none…And is, therefore, less effective. Compromisers are often seen as being poor decision makers and succumb to various pressures.
3. **Benevolent Autocrat**: Uses a high task orientation and a low relationship orientation in a situation where such behaviour is appropriate, and is, therefore, more effective. Benevolent Autocrats are seen as knowing what they want and how to get it.
4. **Autocrat**: Uses a high task orientation and a low relationship orientation in a situation where such behaviour is inappropriate and is, therefore, less effective. Autocrats are seen as having no confidence in others and being interested only in the immediate job.
5. **Developer**: Uses a high relationship orientation and a low task orientation in a situation where such behaviour is appropriate and is, therefore, more effective. Developers are seen to have implicit trust in people and are primarily concerned with the development of individuals.
6. **Missionary**: Uses a high relationship orientation and a low task orientation in a situation where such behaviour is inappropriate and is, therefore, less effective. A missionary is, generally, seen as being interested in harmony.
7. **Bureaucrat**: Uses a low task and relationship orientation in a situation where such behaviour is appropriate and is, therefore, more effective. Bureaucrats are seen as primarily being interested in rules and procedures for their own sake, and desire to maintain control over the situation by their authority.
8. **Deserter**: Uses a low task and a low relationship orientation in a situation where such behaviour is inappropriate and is therefore, less effective. Deserters are seen as uninvolved and passive.

Note: The description given above has been edited and reproduced from materials originally produced by W.J. Reddin and distributed by Organizational Tests Ltd., Canada.

1.3 The Functions of Management

1.3.1 The Purpose of Management is:

To Ensure Results are Achieved

- To achieve results you must:
  - ☑ Develop Insights: Into what a Manager is and does.
  - ☑ Know the Tasks: Managers are required to perform.
  - ☑ Know and Develop: Managerial attitudes and skills.
  - ☑ Know How to make Decisions: This is what Managers do!

1.3.2 Management Tools for being Effective and Achieving Results

- Planning and Organization
  - ☑ Organize yourself, your staff, your activities and your time.
  - ☑ Set Goals.
- Time Management and Delegation
  - ☑ Efficient use of time by avoiding time wasters.
  - ☑ Delegate tasks correctly and responsibly.
- Job Descriptions and Performance Appraisals
  - ☑ Define tasks and responsibilities of each staff member.
  - ☑ Facilitate personnel evaluations: This is a basis for promotions.
  - ☑ Improves performance and increases productivity.
- Problem Solving and Decision Making
  - ☑ Designed to improve the quality of your decisions.
  - ☑ Resolves problems more imaginatively and effectively.
- Leadership and Motivation
  - ☑ To be effective, you must lead and inspire.
  - ☑ Understanding leaders can provide ways to motivate others.
- Effective Communication
  - ☑ The medium through which Managers …manage.

- ☑ Covers written, verbal and non-verbal communication.
- ☑ Includes listening and one-way communication.

- Work Management
  - ☑ Improves the efficiency of your office programme.
  - ☑ Management of office/programme system.

1.4 Leadership Traits

Leadership is the influence that a particular individual exerts upon the goal achievements of others (team members) in an organizational context. In theory, of course, *'influence'* can be exerted by any team member... Thus anyone can engage in *leadership.*

In practice, however, some team members are in a better position to exert influence than others... They are, generally speaking, those assigned with titles like M*anager* or S*upervisor.*

1.4.1 Definition of Leadership

- Effective Leadership: Is when the *influence* is exerted in a manner that achieves organizational goals and enhances satisfaction, innovation, productivity and commitment of team members.
- Ineffective Leadership: Is when, even if the formal title (supervisor, etc.) is assigned, the person fails to exert the *influence* on other team members.

1.4.2 The Traits Associated with the Effectiveness Leadership

What is a trait? Most people say traits are: Personal characteristics of an individual such as physical attributes (pretty, tall), intellectual ability (clear thinking, analytical mind) and personality.

However, not all personal traits can be associated with good leadership.

- Keeping good hygiene doesn't necessarily make you a good leader, but it's an essential trait to have.

- Being funny doesn't always mean you are a good leader… It might make you appear like a nice guy but may or may not contribute to your leadership abilities.

1.4.3 Traits that are often related to leadership

- ☑ Intelligence
- ☑ Energy
- ☑ Enthusiasm
- ☑ Pervasiveness
- ☑ Motivation to Lead
- ☑ Emotional Stability
- ☑ Honesty and Integrity
- ☑ Effective Communication
- ☑ Need for Achievement

…but just possessing these traits does not necessarily mean you are an effective leader…

1.4.4 Behaviours of Leadership

As this handbook is designed for Managers and Directors, we will discuss the behaviour of the formal, or assigned leader (Manager/Supervisor) only, and not the informal leader. In this section on behaviours, we will also look at the critical behaviours leaders engage in, and, try to see how these behaviours influence the performance and satisfaction of the team members.

1.4.5 Two Basic Kinds of Behaviours in Leadership

- **Consideration**: The extent to which a leader is approachable and shows personal concern for other team members. The considerate leader is seen as:
- Friendly >>Egalitarian >> Protective of the team's welfare
- **Initiating Structure**: The degree to which a leader concentrates on group (team) goal attainment. The structuring leader is seen as the one who:
- Stresses procedures >> Schedules work >> Assigns tasks

1.4.6 Comments on These Behaviours and Effects on Leadership

Theoretically, consideration and initiating structure behaviours are not incompatible. Presumably, a leader could be high, low or average on one or both behaviours, and still be an effective leader. However, you may assume that a leader who is high in all dimensions will be a more effective leader.

Other situations that affect these behaviours include characteristics of the task, team members and situation (setting). Taking these consequences into play, a leader who is high both in consideration and initiating structuring may not always perform better than others.

Bottom Line: Leadership styles need to keep changing.

1.5 The Result Based Management (RBM)

For the past 6-8 years now donors, spearheaded by the World Bank among others, have insisted that governments and implementing organizations show or *produce evidence* of results from the funds these organizations have been providing for the projects. They **call this approach Results Based Management (RBM)**...or sometimes also referred to as **Evidence Based Management**.

NO longer will donors accept...as a measurement of achievement...statements that objectives have been reached, or evaluation comments claiming that project goals have been met. Donors now want tangible results and proof, verified proof, that their funding has produced *some results*.

The RBM approach is now widely accepted and has pretty much replaced a previous approach **Management by Objectives (MBO)**. The two still interface with each other, but have distinct differences.

More on RBM is provided in part 2, point 10 of this chapter.

1. Differences between RBM and MBO

To understand the strengths of RBM, one should know the differences between Management by Objectives (MBO) and the Results Based Management (RBM) approach clearly.

S. No.	MBO	RBM
1	Measures Performance.	Measures Change.
2	Focus is on setting objectives.	Focus is on achieving results.
3	Details how to achieve objectives.	Details on proof of results.
4	More of a monitoring process.	More of an evaluation process.

By now you are familiarised with the definitions of management styles and the functions of management styles. However, as a Manager you need to know some basic tools, which will assist you in carrying out your responsibilities.

In the following chapters, we are going to provide you with those tools, but we want you to always remember:

Management is not an exact science, and there are no right or wrong answers. Likewise, management styles, traits and tools have different interpretations... The choice is yours to make!

2

Management 'Tips and Tools'

2.1 Management 'Tips'

Might even bring a smile or two!

- There are two groups of people in this world...The first group which does the work and the second group which takes credit for the work. My suggestion is, you try to be in the first group as it is less crowded!
- Delegation of Responsibilities requires that you trust others.
- Negotiations require: Truth, Clarity, and a Sense of Humour.
- A policy consists of four elements:
  - ☑ A principle (basis).
  - ☑ Recurring Situation.
  - ☑ A guide (thought and action of what to do); and
  - ☑ Reference (mention) of the objective (what you want to achieve).
- Ham and eggs... A day's work for a chicken, a lifetime commitment for a pig!
- If you are not making mistakes, then you are not doing anything!
- Any objective must be set in light of all known existing conditions (funds, policies, time, etc.).
- Disappointments are like road bumps – they slow you down a bit but, you enjoy the smooth road afterwards.
- Even if you are on the right track, you will get run over if you just sit there!

- Leadership involves, going beyond formal role requirements to influence others.
- Leadership is a choice…not a position!
- The boss isn't always right…but s/he is always the boss!
- Committees are people who keep minutes and waste hours!
- Name two days of the week that start with the letter 'T'. Most people will quickly say…Tuesday and Thursday…On the other hand, I was thinking the answer was **today** and **tomorrow**… Often more than one answer to the question… Often more than one solution to the problem!
- Management is not an exact science… There are no right or wrong answers!
- The world is run by those who show up!
- There is plenty of room at the top, but no place to sit down!
- Be nice to the people you meet on the way up the ladder of success…as you may need them again on your way down.
- It is nice to be important, but it is more important to be nice!
- When you start to throw dirt, you start to lose ground!
- Be strong, be firm, be decisive, be *mean* if needed, but don't be an arrogant jerk about it!!
- If you don't intend to listen, then don't ask!
- Know the way, go the way, show the way!
- There are three groups of people in the world: The one percent who makes things happen, the two percent who watch things happening, and the ninety seven percent who have no idea what is happening.
- It is better to ask *dumb questions* than make *dumb mistakes*!
- Fall down seven times, get up eight!
- You're either a part of the problem or part of the solution!
- If you always do what you've always done, then you'll always get what you always got!
- If something is not worth doing at all, then it is not worth doing well!

- Figure out what you don't like doing. Then stop doing it.
- What counts is what you know after you know it all!

Note: None of the above quotes are the original idea of the author, and have been taken from a variety of sources. The origination/true author for any of the above quotes is not known to the author of The Undressed Manager.

2.2 Some Management 'Tools'

2.2.1. Decision Making

<u>Overview</u>

Decision Making is a daily task of a Programme Director or Manager. It is the Manager/Director, who, ultimately, has to take the **responsibility** and make the decision.

There are different styles used in Decision Making with the most common styles identified as – **autocratic, consultative and participative**. Your decision making style will include:

FACTORS
• That pertain to you, your values and your attitudes.
• That pertain to your subordinates, their expectations and their development needs.
• That pertain to the task, complexity, specialization; and
• That pertain to the organization, time pressures and encouragement of the staff, etc.

Here are six ways of making a decision:

1. Manager decides;
2. *Manager sells* his/her decision to the group;
3. Manager announces the decision and permits questions from the group;
4. Manager presents tentative decision... Consults the group, then decides
5. Manager presents the problem... Asks the group for ideas and then decides; or

6. Manager gives complete (full) permission to the group to define the problem and then permits the group to make the final decision.

Making decisions is an important management function, and as we mentioned earlier, is the responsibility of the Manager/Director. The *'boss'* should not shirk this responsibility. However, and, depending on the management style of the Manager/Director, decision making is something that can be delegated…With some conditions. These conditions will depend on the Decision Making style adopted.

In the overview above, we briefly described the Decision Making styles… Autocratic, consultative, participative. Now, let's see if we can help you identify what style of Decision Making you practice with this simple exercise.

Exercise

I'm going to ask you to write down three different decisions that you have made recently. Then I would like you to indicate the style you used (see decision-making styles below) to make that decision. All you have to do is look at your decision, and then indicate how you made that decision by marking an 'X' by the style...or the closest style. An analysis of your decision making style can be found in the paragraph following the exercise.

To begin the Decision Making exercise please recall three recent decisions you have made at work, write them down, and then put an 'X' next to the corresponding number of the decision making style (or the closest style) that you used in making the decision.

S. No.	DECISION-MAKING STYLE	DECISION NUMBER
1	Did you make the decision independently using only the information available to you at the time?	1___2___3___
2	Did you make the decision independently, but, after obtaining the necessary information from your subordinates?	1___2___3___
3	Did you consult the appropriate subordinates individually to obtain ideas/suggestions before making the decision?	1___2___3___
4	Did you consult your subordinates as a group to obtain ideas/suggestions before making the decision?	1___2___3___
5	Did you join your subordinates as a group and make a decision, which had the support of the whole group?	1___2___3___

Remember:

Each decision you make may have a different style. Also, it is possible for you to start out in one style in making the decision and shift to another (i.e. begin autocratic and shift into a participative or consultative style).

Recap of Decision Making

Now, before we give you the analysis let's remind you that the section above has been describing Decision Making styles. We have discussed the different styles: autocratic, consultative and participative, and how you may use one or a combination of these styles in your decision making process. The above section has also brought to your attention the fact that you may start with one style of decision making and then shift into another (i.e., start out in an autocratic manner and end up being participative before making the final decision). This is fairly common.

Another way to make decisions, that isn't scientific at all, but is fast and convenient, is the old **advantage and disadvantage method**.

Simply put the word *advantage* at the top left corner of a piece of paper and the word *disadvantage* at the top right hand corner of the same paper, as shown below. This example is helping you to make the decision about finding a new job.

ADVANTAGE	DISADVANTAGE
(i) More money. (ii) New responsibilities. (iii) Improved chances of promotion.	(i) Have to move to another city. (ii) Have to learn new procedures. (iii) Have to adjust to new boss.

After you have completed the list, you can weigh the advantages against disadvantages to see what decision you should make. If there are more advantages than disadvantages, then you will probably take the new job offer…Too many disadvantages and you will stay where you are.

But also, what you should factor into this method of making a decision is the *level of importance* of each response. Even if the total number of advantages are more than the disadvantages, you may still decide not to take the new job because disadvantages of your, leaving your hometown may *out weigh* advantages of taking the new job.

For example, although you make more money, social obligations and income taxes are higher, thus your net salary is actually less than what you are now making.

Analysis of your Decision Making exercise

As promised, the analysis of your three different decisions. If you applied:-

Style 1 and/or 2, this indicates you are using an **autocratic** style of decision making;

Style 3 and/or 4 indicate a **consultative** approach and;

Style 5 uses a **participative** method to make a decision.

But, you may have guessed these styles already by the keywords!!!!

As a final note on Decision Making, please remember that it is usually the programme Manager/Director who must ultimately make the final decision, and that, decisions must be made...The process can often be hard, painful and even emotional.

2.2.2. Problem Solving (note change here in number)

The ability to deal with problems effectively is a major requirement of management. The responsibility and challenge for the Manager/Director is to find the most appropriate solution.

When faced with a problem, some Managers react with a quick decision and provide an obvious answer to the problem...Which is not necessarily the best solution. There is usually more than one possible answer to any problem.

Exploring ways and generating alternative solutions to a problem involves **creative thinking**...and selecting the best solution requires **analytical thinking**. Combining the two *thinking* processes improves the quality of your decisions and resolves the problems more imaginatively and effectively.

There are several parts of problem solving:

- Define the problem clearly... State the causes and consequences of the problem (defining the actual problem is not always easy).
- For creative thinking it's best to organize small groups to generate solutions.
- Then select the best solution (result of analytical thinking).
- And once you have the solution determine a plan to solve the problem.

Steps in Problem Solving

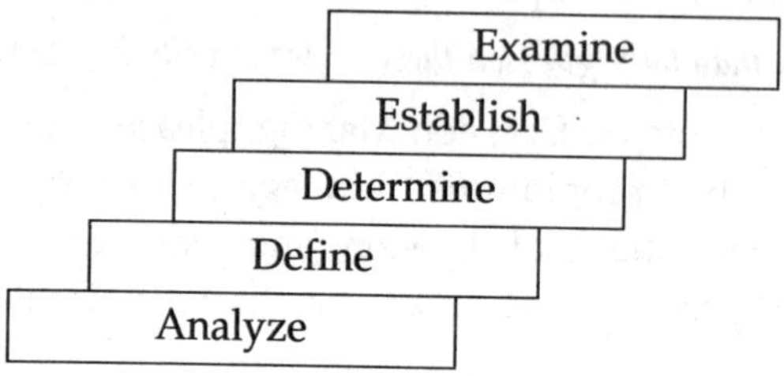

1. **Analyze** the problem as stated and collect information about the problem...Who says it is a problem; when did it become a problem; where does the problem occur?
2. **Define** the problem in writing. A problem is an obstacle/barrier, blocking you from reaching your objective... Write it down, look at it and then ask yourself what is the present situation and how do I wish to change it?
3. **Determine** the consequences of the problem...Will it happen again if nothing is done; how severe are the consequences... Perhaps you just ignore it?
4. **Establish** the cause of the problem... Ask yourself what are the factors involved; can you overcome the cause and what resources do you need?
5. **Examine** the situation and identify clearly/accurately the obstacle or obstacles which are preventing you from moving forward... The challenge is how to overcome the obstacles.

Finding Solutions

Some Managers will tell you that identifying the problem is the hard part... Others believe that finding ways to solve the problem is the real task. For sure there is no crystal ball for finding solutions, but perhaps the following table will help you. By answering the questions, with a yes or no, in columns 2, 3 and 4 below, you might find a solution for solving the problem...or at least this analysis will provide you with some direction for finding a solution.

Column 1	Column 2	Column 3	Column 4
Resource	**Needed Resource (Is the resource needed ?) Yes or No**	**Resource Available (Is it possible to divert it?) Yes or No**	**Resource Not Available (Is it possible to acquire it?) Yes or No**
Personnel			
Money			
Equipment			
Facilities			
Time			
Knowledge			
Skills			
Political Influence			
Reputation			
Legitimacy			
Energy			
Control over Information			

After completing the above table, you should have enough information to make an informed decision...and hopefully, come up with a solution. Of course, you have to answer the questions honestly and with due consideration. Unrealistic response to the above questions will not produce a realistic solution.

2.2.3. Delegation

Delegation is a way for you to improve "efficiency" and increase "productivity".

<u>**Overview**</u>

Through proper delegation you will achieve more (outputs) with the resources (inputs) you have available with you. Delegation is the means by which a Manager or programme Director can achieve results **by giving responsibility, authority and opportunity to others** to carry out the tasks more efficiently for which a Manager or programme Director is ultimately accountable.

Example: A programme Director must prepare a quarterly report. S/he can delegate the collection of data or assign sections of the report to be completed by a subordinate, BUT the programme Director must retain ultimate responsibility for producing, content and control of the report.(changes made here in wording)

What is delegation?

Delegation is achieving results by giving responsibility to others.

Why should you delegate?

- To save your time.
- To motivate other staff/team members.
- To develop staff skills.
- To create more efficient operations.

When should you delegate?

- When someone else can do the job more efficiently.
- At a particular time, like, when you are busy.

How to delegate?

- Select the right person… Don't delegate a task to someone if s/he can't do the job correctly.
- Delegate in advance… Don't wait till the last minute or until there is a problem before you delegate.
- Delegate for specific results… Know what outcome you want when you delegate a task.
- Explain to the person, in detail, what you require and how you plan to use the outcome.
- Delegate gradually… Don't delegate too much, too fast.

What happens when you delegate?

There are several important things to remember when you delegate.

We mentioned earlier that, when you delegate you give *responsibility, authority and opportunity* to others. When you delegate you should be aware of certain attitudes or behaviour change that you must accept. They include:

- A willingness to accept the result and consequences of the work delegated.
- A willingness to let others make mistakes.
- A willingness to trust others!
- A willingness to let go.

What work should not be delegated?

As a Manager or programme Director there are some tasks you should not delegate. They include:

- Direct assignments that YOU have been given by your superiors.
- Overall programme planning and budgeting
- Solving moral problems.
- Coaching and developing skills of others.
- Staff performance appraisals/evaluations.
- Confidential work.

2.2.4. Motivation

Motivation is the persistent 'effort' put forth by the staff/team member to complete a task and reach his/her project goal.

Overview

Motivation is a traditional topic discussed in most organizations...and a tool that is used by Managers/Programme Directors usually to increase productivity of the organization or compensate for the changes and demands of the organization.

A couple of common mistakes made by programme Managers, when using motivation as a management tool, are:

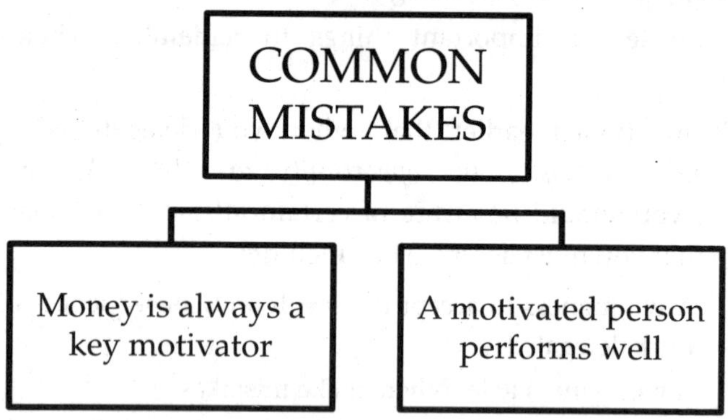

Money is not always the key motivating factor for people... There are many other things to consider, like job satisfaction, working environment. Also, many Managers believe if team member is motivated, s/he will perform well... This is not necessarily true. Performance depends on other things such as...skill levels, aptitude, understanding of tasks...and not just motivation alone.

There is no single motivational technique that can be applied across the board by programme Managers.

What motivates people?

A possible first step you can take is to find out *what actually motivates your staff/team*. You can try to determine what motivates them by administering the following exercise. Remember there is no right or wrong answer in management... And the responses given by each employee is your first *hint* on how you can motivate them in the future.

Exercise

The questions in this exercise should be answered by an individual staff/team member by circling 'A' (meaning s/he agrees with the statement) or 'DA' (meaning s/he disagrees with the statement.

S. No.	Questions	Response: A/DA
1	Anyone is able to do almost any job if s/he tries hard enough.	A/DA
2	Most employees are interested in doing work of which they can be proud of.	A/DA
3	Lack of interest accounts for more loafing on part of the staff/team member than does laziness.	A/DA

4	A staff member's ability to do a given piece of work is always a sure sign that the staff member is satisfied and properly placed.	A/DA
5	The motivating factor amongst most employees is to be paid at the end of the week and to be told what to do.	A/DA
6	A staff member's attitude has little effect on his/her production.	A/DA
7	The best way to get the most work from staff members is to make them feel like they might lose their job.	A/DA
8	High wages and job security are the only things important to staff members.	A/DA

How to Analyze a Motivational Problem:

Most Managers/Programme Directors often associate poor (low) performance with poor (low) motivation...which is not necessarily true. The programme Manager should determine if non-performance is a result of low motivation...or if there are some other causes. The following steps on how to analyze a motivational problem should help you decide if motivation is the problem.

To determine if non-performance is the result of poor motivation, the Programme Manager must *eliminate* the following four possibilities that can affect job performance. After eliminating these possibilities if performance of the staff member is still poor (low) then the problem might be motivation.

1. **Problem of Communication**... Is there a misperception on part of the staff member on what is expected? Is there a language or cultural problem?
2. **Problem of Ability**... Can the person do the assigned task? Does the staff member lack physical or mental ability to undertake the assigned task?

3. **Problem of Training**... Is the person trained sufficiently to do the job? An improperly trained staff member will never get the job done...regardless of the staff member's motivation.
4. **Problem of Opportunity**... The staff member may know how to do the assigned task, but is held back by the surroundings or work environment...or it could be lack of proper tools, equipment or outdated computer software.

Staff and team members must be motivated and it is the responsibility of the Manager/programme Director to motivate them.

Some ideas at no cost to your project or organization....

Below are some ideas on how to motivate people:

- Give positive feedback on performance.
- Give praise.
- Give the staff member the work activities s/he would prefer.
- Assign work activities that are typically performed by supervisors.
- Acknowledge their work openly in newsletters/reports.
- Send the staff member for training programmes.
- Give the staff member an opportunity to train others.
- Give letters of recommendation and put them in personal file.
- Provide special or better work places (near a window/own room).

- Provide an opportunity to be recognized by senior organization leaders.
- Provide special desk accessories, new computer monitor.
- Redecorate his/her office.
- Ask him/her for ideas and/or thoughts on work related matters.
- Share with the staff member words of praise/satisfaction from superiors.
- Give promotions.
- Rotate job assignments.

Some factors that can adversely affect staff motivation:

☑ Lack of achievement in doing the job (for whatever reason).
☑ Absence of adequate recognition for doing a good job.
☑ Lack of advancement/promotion.
☑ Lack of increased responsibility.
☑ Dissatisfaction with the work/job itself.
☑ The incompetence of the supervisor/Manager.
☑ Lack of friendliness of the supervisor/Manager.
☑ Certain policies of the organization.
☑ Improper organisational administration.
☑ Lack of clear-cut Job Description.
☑ Poor pay/fringe benefits.
☑ Inadequate growth/advancement potential.
☑ Lack of support/credit for good ideas.
☑ Job insecurity.
☑ Poor peer relations.

And the ultimate suggestion on motivation...

So far, this handbook has been very intense, and so I thought what we needed was **not** another serious paragraph, but something that could lift our spirits a bit. Therefore, I looked up some-things on motivation. The following is a little numerical quiz that will give us some help on motivation as well as, unfortunately, a lesson in life. Enjoy!!!

Did you ever wonder about those people, usually your Manager or Directors, who are always saying "we want staff and team members who can give more than 100%." In fact I want a staff that can give me 103 % or even more…blah, blah, blah! Well, here is a mathematical "tip", which might help you meet your boss's expectation.

Step 1: Give the English alphabet a numerical value as follows (A=1; B=2; C=3; etc).:

A	B	C	D	E	F	G	H	I	J
1	2	3	4	5	6	7	8	9	10

K	L	M	N	O	P	Q	R	S	T
11	12	13	14	15	16	17	18	19	20

U	V	W	X	Y	Z
21	22	23	24	25	26

Step 2: Figure out how to give more than 100% as follows:

>>>H A R D W O R K (always a good way)…Write H=8; A=1;R=18…and add the total number value

8 1 18 4 23 15 18 11 = 98 % …close to 100%, But…now try

A T T I T U D E (another good feature)… Write A=1; T= 20; T= 20…and again add the total number value

1 20 20 9 20 21 4 5 = 100%…But we asked for more than 100% So.....

Step 3: Now you are at 100% … To get more than 100% figure out the answer by putting correct letters to the numbers given below:

1 19 19 11 9 19 19 9 14 7 = 118 %

Did you get the answer? Now you know what is required to get ahead?

2.2.5. Group and Team Building

A sociologist would define a group as two or more people interacting independently to achieve a common goal.

Overview

In the implementation of your programmes, as well as in our daily conversation, we talk of informal or formal groups, special interest groups, ethnic and even radical groups. **Interaction** is the basic aspect of a group...Either you are or you aren't in a group. It's like being pregnant...Either you are or you aren't!

Previously, interaction was verbal and face-to-face, but with fax machines, and even more so with the intranet, people can interact and yet be miles apart.

Formal Work Groups are groups (teams) that organizations establish to facilitate achievement of organizational goals. The most common formal group consists of a superior authority and subordinates (a work team), who report to that superior. Other formal groups can be, a task force or a committee, but these are usually for a specific purpose, or temporary.

Organizations can, and usually do, have **Informal Groups**, that emerge naturally in response to the common interests of organizational members. Informal groups can either help or hurt an organization depending on their norms or behaviour. It is the **Formal Work Group** that we will focus on during this section of the handbook, keeping in mind, however, that informal groups do have an influence on the team.

The Work Group

The work group has tasks, roles and is organized to perform:

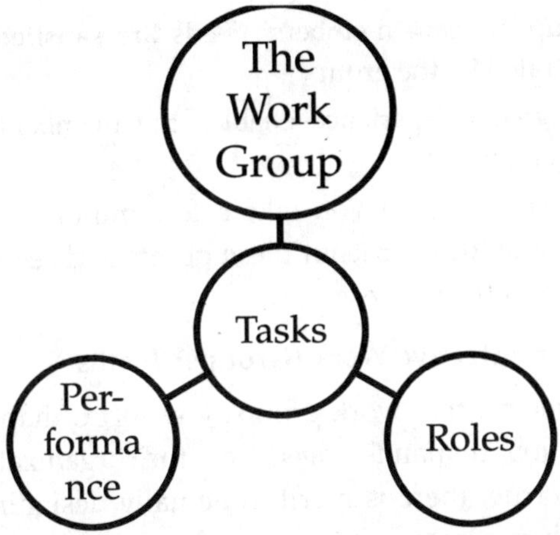

Tasks: These will vary as some tasks will be measured where group performance is dependent upon the sum of the performance of individual group members (additive tasks), or other tasks that will be measured by the performance of the best group member (disjunctive tasks).

Roles: There are generally two types of roles in an organization: (1) Designated (assigned), which basically defines *who does what;* and (2) Emergent roles; roles that develop naturally to meet the socio-emotional needs of a group. An *old pro* may emerge from within a group to assist other group members in learning their job... The group clown is another example of an emergent role.

Performance: Performance of the group (team) is most often what a Manager/Director is interested in...and whether the group is effective or ineffective.

What Do We Mean by Effective?

A work group or a team is effective when:

- Its physical or intellectual output combines the honesty of the team with the needs of management to achieve the organization's objectives.

- Group or team members' needs are satisfied rather than frustrated by the group.
- The group experience enables the members to continue working together.

I would suggest that you take a few minutes, before going on, and review with your team these points and see if you are on track to achieve effectiveness.

The Design of Effective Work (Groups) Teams

Most of us believe that work groups just sort of happen...out of response to job demands, needs or the organization's goals. While this is true, there is merit in actually designing the work group, and being more creative in the group's organizational structure. If the work group is designed then there are creative ways also to manage this group. The notion of designing a work group is a little revolutionary, but has scope. Effective work groups are like a sports team... Sports teams are really small groups made up of highly skilled individuals who are able to meld (join) these skills into a cohesive effort.

Effective Work Teams

In this section, we will look at the design, operations and management of effective work teams. The following paragraphs will focus more on the **design** of these work groups/teams, with some mention of different operating styles of these groups.

The two most common styles are – **the self-managed work team and the cross-functional team**. With self-managed teams you have an opportunity to do challenging work under reduced supervision, whereas the cross-functional team brings people with different functional specialties together, in an effort to invent, design or deliver a product (or service) better.

Now take a look at your staff/team and determine...**What style do you come under in your place of work**? Are you 'self-managed' or a 'cross-functional' team? As Managers/Directors you are interested in reaching the highest level of effectiveness from your work groups/teams.

An Example of an effective work group

The example we will use is a sports team. It goes without saying:

A successful sports team equals an effective work group.

When we look at a sports team what do we see?

- In most cases the teams are small (small groups).
- They are usually highly skilled (talented) individuals.
- Who are able to meld their skills into a cohesive effort.
- They are intrinsically motivating.
- Provide very direct feedback.
- If there are status differences, the basis for these differences is contribution.
- The team is obsessive about obtaining the right personnel.
- Tryouts are offered in an effort to obtain the right players; and
- A team is "coached" not supervised.

Can you see the similarities between a sports team and your working group?

Can you equate your work group with the characteristics of a sports team? One example might be a sports tryout. A tryout is the same, or at least similar, to a job interview. Can you think of some others? Do you see how a good sports team makes an effective work group?

Another example:

A sports team uses (melds) the individual athletic ability (skills) in a joint (cohesive) way to win the game. Don't working teams/groups do the same thing? Can you discuss this with your staff/group and find other parallels?

Personal Behaviour in a Group

As we discussed above, teams/groups are formed from individuals, and it is the skills of the individuals joined together that makes an effective working group or team. The team is designed to perform and complete a task. We think that in order to understand the team, the Manager/Director must first understand the behaviour of the individuals. Also, it is good for the individual to understand, and even question his/her behaviour, as a member of this team/group. The following exercise will perhaps help you think about your behaviour as part of a team/group.

Exercise

Analysis of Personal Behaviour in Groups:

All of us are a part of a team or group at some point in our work life. We are also members of committees and/or participate in staff meetings...These can be considered as groups/teams too. To explore personal behaviour in a group the following exercise is offered. This exercise is divided into two parts: the first part exams your behaviour and the second part asks you to think about possible changes to your behaviour.

Part 1: Read each question carefully and then tick or circle the number that best describes your usual behaviour in a group.

Part 2: After ticking or circling the number, pick out 3 or 4 areas which you would most like to change your behaviour and then draw an arrow pointing in which direction you desire your behaviour to change.

*Q 1: **Ability** to listen to others in an understanding way.*

(low, don't hear) (average) (highly receptive)

0 1 2 3 4 5 6 7

*Q 2: **Ability** to influence others in the group.*

(no influence) (average) (highly influential)

0 1 2 3 4 5 6 7

Q 3:. Tendency to build on the previous ideas of other group members.

(never/infrequent) (average) (very frequent)

0 1 2 3 4 5 6 7

Q 4: Likely to trust others.

(guard myself) (average) (expose myself)

0 1 2 3 4 5 6 7

Q 5: Willingness to be influenced by others.

(resistant) (average) (very willing)

0 1 2 3 4 5 6 7

Q 6: Tendency to run the group.

(low) (average) (take control)

0 1 2 3 4 5 6 7

Q 7: Awareness of the feelings of others.

(unaware) (average) (very sensitive)

0 1 2 3 4 5 6 7

Q 8: The degree of my understanding of why I do what I do.

(low self insight) (average) (high insight)

0 1 2 3 4 5 6 7

Q 9: Reaction to conflict and antagonism in the group.

(low tolerance) (average) (welcome it)

0 1 2 3 4 5 6 7

Q 10: Reaction to opinions opposed to mine.

(low tolerance) (average) (welcome them)

0 1 2 3 4 5 6 7

Being Effective

From a review of this Group and Team Building section we have learned:

1. Individual behaviours are important within a group.
2. We begin to see how different groups (formal, ethnic, etc.) are formed;
3. And the role they play in building a team.

What Managers are really looking for from a group/team is the effectiveness of the group. The Manager is expected to achieve or produce results by his/her supervisors. A Manager pays a salary to his/her staff/team to be effective and produce results.

How to Make the Teams more Effective

Self-Managed Teams

Most of the development organizations (NGOs, government) follow a style of self-managed teams. Occasionally, you may have a group of consultants coming in to help you design a programme (a cross-functional style), but mostly it will be self-managed. We could also point out here to refer back to the section on Delegation (Part 2, Point 3 of this Chapter), which is so important in self-management teams.

Key Points — To look at in self-managed group/teams:

- The tasks assigned should be complex, challenging but significant.
- The group/team should perform the task from beginning to end.
- The group/team must have something useful to manage.
- Self-managed teams require considerable interaction and cohesiveness.
- The members must be trusting, understanding and stable.
- The Manager should ensure the group size is right.
- Coordination of tasks and allocation of tasks is critical – who is responsible?
- The group requires a level of expertise, but the group, as a whole, should be able to complete the tasks…which doesn't mean that each individual has to know everything; and
- The group/team should have members who are similar enough to work together well, yet diverse enough (skills/perspectives) to achieve the task.

Barriers to Effective Group Working

As with everything in life, there are some barriers or obstacles in the management of programmes. It is up to the Manager to find ways to overcome these barriers, decide when the group or team approach should not be used and when the Manager must act alone. Knowing how to overcome these barriers and when to use the right strategy will make you a better Manager.

At times when the group/team is not working together well or effectively to achieve the group task, the reason may be the existence of one, or more, of the following barriers:

1. Lack of agreement on objectives
   - The objectives are not explicit/clear.
   - Difference of opinion on the objectives among group members.
   - Hidden agendas.
   - Different levels of commitment within the group.
2. Lack of agreement on constraints
   - Reasons why things aren't being done :
   - Time—insufficient time to plan, to complete the tasks.
   - Authority and resource constraints on authority and resource approvals.
   - Information—lack of data/research findings, delay in policies.
3. Lack of agreement on decision making
   - Who is in-charge, who's right?
   - Authority--who has it, who gave it.
   - Vocal minority—are their arguments delaying the process.
   - Majority—Is the majority always right, why not move forward then?
   - Consensus—can you reach one-why not, who or what is the barrier.
4. Ineffective communication
   - What is the problem, who can/should solve it?
   - Poor listening--will training help, what else is needed?
   - Interruptions—time management, good planning may help.
   - Lack of continuity—change in group/team members.
   - Ambiguity—insignificant tasks, unclear objectives.

Strategies for using Authority

The following examples are by no means a complete list, but do highlight who is the *appropriate authority* at specific times and under what circumstances the decision should be made.

To use the chart below, first locate the decision maker at the top of the chart. There are three choices of authority:

- It is the Manager alone who will decide.
- The Manager with one of his/her staff playing active role.
- The Manager decides with the whole group.

Then look at the factors, which are listed in the first column. Now you must match the factors with the appropriate authority.

How to use this chart correctly?

An example

Let's look at the 'TIME' factor first, and ask yourself the question: ... Is time a factor in making the decision? If yes, the factor is 'TIME'... Then perhaps the Manager could decide alone if time is not available (in his/her assessment) to ask others.

But if s/he determines that there **is** sufficient time, before the decision has to be made, to ask others then time is NOT the factor, and another choice of authority can be selected. The *amount of time* available before the decision has to be made is also a factor to consider.

FACTORS	MANAGER DECIDES ALONE	MANAGER AND ONE STAFF DECIDE	MANAGER CONSULTS THE WHOLE TEAM
	When	When	When
TIME	Not available	Available	Available
TECHNICAL KNOW-HOW	Has full know-how	Needs help in technical areas	Needs help in technical areas
JUDGEMENTAL COMPETENCE	Fully competent	Needs help to fill gaps in competence	Needs help to fill gaps in competence
CAN OTHERS ADD ANYTHING TO THE DECISION	NO (should not decide alone)	YES	YES

WHOSE PROBLEM	Manager's alone	Staff member's	Group problem
WILL ACCEPT SUGGESTIONS	NO	YES	YES
WILL IT HELP OTHERS TO CARRY OUT THE PROJECT IF THEY ARE INVOLVED	NO (should not decide alone)	YES	YES
COORDINATION OF EFFORT	Not needed	Vertical (boss or subordinate)	Horizontal needed
LEARNING VALUE	No value	Value to one	Value-to group
FOLLOW-UP	Not necessary	Necessary	Necessary

2.2.6. Strategic Management

Strategies are forging of the organization's goals, setting of objectives and formulation of policies for proper implementation of the programme.

Overview

A strategy is an action taken by a Manager to offset actual or potential actions. It is the means used to achieve the ends (objectives), and is a unified plan that ties all parts of an organization together.

A strategy begins with a concept of how to use the available resources most effectively.

Strategic management can be described as **a process** by which the organization's missions, purposes, objectives, strategies, policies and action programmes are formulated (designed), evaluated, implemented and guided **so that the end results of the organization are achieved.**

Now that's a real mouthful of words to digest…and we hope it is clear as strategies are extremely important for all aspects of programme management. Donors are increasingly asking for your *project's strategic planning*...or your strategy for sustainability. May be you need to read the words above, one more time, before you go further, although there are some examples given later that might clear away the 'fuzziness'...if there is any.

Formulating Strategies

As the Manager or Director, it is your job to develop a planning framework to administer strategies of your organization. An overall strategy for your organization will consist of four stages:

Four Stages of Strategy Development	
1.	Formulation of the overall organizational strategy.
2.	Strategy integration into the functional areas.
3.	Strategy implementation.
4.	Periodic evaluation and reformulation of strategy.

The first stage – formulation of overall strategy – is really a type of long range planning. Strategic management begins with formulating your organization's strategy, which will include your management philosophy and objectives.

Determinants of Formulating a Strategy

There are four main determinants of strategy formulation:

Four Determinants of a Strategy	
1.	Philosophy of Manager/Director.
2.	Mission/objectives of the organization.
3.	The Manager's/Director's perception (reading) of the external factors, forces and events affecting the organization.
4.	The Manager's/Director's perception (reading) of the internal environment, resources (human/financial) and functions of the organization.

There may be others, but these four usually determine the overall purpose, related strategies and policies of the organization.

Policy Development

What is a policy? A policy is a general statement, made by the organization, which serves as a **guide** to **thought** (what you would like to have done or do) and **action** (how to do it) for a recurring situation. A policy statement facilitates the achievement of the objective.

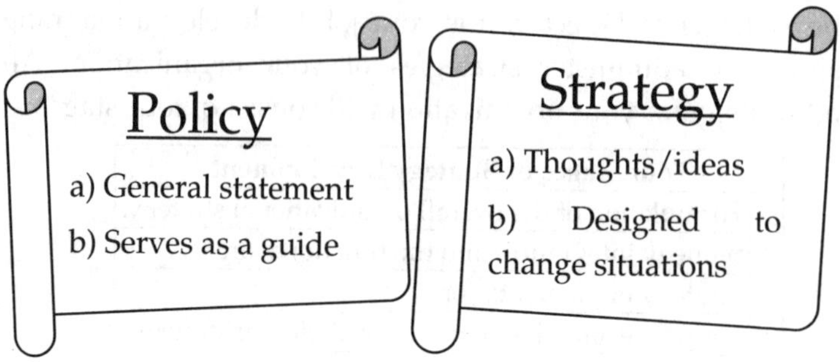

Question: Which comes first…Policy or Strategy?

Example: The organization's strategy is to provide a healthy work environment in the office. To achieve this objective one of our policies could be *no smoking inside the office building*.

Differences between a policy and a strategy:

A strategy (thought/idea) is usually determined by the Manager/Director and sets down what s/he wants to do (achieve). After the strategy is set in motion, and is working well, it usually becomes a policy (statement). A rule of thumb…strategies are designed to change situations and policies are designed for recurring situations. Strategies are general…while policies are specific and the guide (path or direction) that should be followed.

Policies and strategies are closely related and are often used interchangeably.

Exercise

As Manager/Director, you want to develop a good programme team. To do this you must develop a set of policies. First on your list are personnel policies, which include setting individual goals. Incorporating the four elements of policy development, (shown above) make a personnel policy on goal setting for your team members.

Hint: First develop a strategy (what do you want to do) and then develop the policy around what you want to achieve, and what is possible in the given environment.

Value Sets

The Manager or Director has, as we have stated throughout this handbook, a particular **management style**. S/he will also have a philosophy (values) of how to manage, which can be influenced by different sets of values. Knowing and understanding the philosophy of the Manager/Director is very important. Given below is a list of different value sets that may influence a Manager/Director's management style and enter into his/her decision making, problem solving and programme vision.

Different types of Value Sets	
Social	Legal
Economic	Religious
Technological	Ethical
Political	Aesthetic

Two questions:

1. How many of the value sets your Manager/Director possess?
2. Which value sets do you feel are most important for your Manager/Director to have? Why??

2.2.7. Sustainability

A project is said to be sustainable when it can continue to operate and function after the initial donor's financial support has stopped.

Overview

People generally think of sustainability in financial terms only. However, there are often non-financial matters, like a well trained/skilled staff…who is available and ready to perform project activities without additional inputs. This is a degree/level of sustainability. When you are evaluating your programmes, you can try to show different types of sustainability… You don't have to focus on financial sustainability only.

You can also consider technological or behavioural sustainability, which is as important as financial sustainability. We will cover other levels of sustainability in this section...and the good news is some donors are now accepting this thinking as well!

Example:

In sustainability one must always be thinking and trying to find ways of doing more…and we often have to **'think outside the box'** as demonstrated in the example below.

You are driving down the road in your car on a wild, stormy night, when you pass by a bus stop and you see three people waiting for the bus.

1. An old lady who looks as if she is about to die.
2. An old friend who once saved your life.
3. The perfect partner you have been dreaming about.

Which one would you choose to offer a ride to, knowing that there could only be one passenger in your car. Think before you continue reading.

This is a moral/ethical dilemma that was once actually used as a part of job application. You could pick up the old lady because she is going to die, and thus you could save her first. Or you could take the old friend because he once saved your life, and this would be the perfect chance to pay him back. However, you may never be able to find your perfect mate again.

The person who was hired for the job simply answered: He would give the car's keys to his old friend and let him drive the old lady to the hospital. He would simply stay behind and wait for the next bus with the partner of his dream.

Sometimes, we gain more if we are able to give up our stubborn thought limitations. Sustainability is going to be hard to achïeve... So always remember to think outside the box.

Donors and Sustainability

Sustainability is one of the first questions asked by donors when reviewing your proposal...and they usually take a very hard look at this issue. They will ask, what will happen when our funding runs out...and will the programme be able to continue if we can no longer support your efforts? These are hard questions and ones you will have to address as a Manager.

When I was a Programme Manager and was asked this question, my first response was to try to assure the donor that sustainability is important, and that, by applying my management skills to a well designed project we will try to reach the highest level of sustainability...both in the short and long term. Then move on to explain some ways in which the programme should be and can be made sustainable, at least over the next three to five year period.

What you can explain or point out is that **nothing will ever be 100% sustainable** that things change during implementation and as the Manager/Director you will begin to immediately look at **degrees or levels of sustainability**. A certain percentage (degree) of your programme will always be sustainable, I believe, especially if you have developed a strong local structure and can get by with local inputs/resources. Mention that you will closely manage recurring costs and maximize the capital investment costs made by the donor.

Approaching Sustainability in Different Ways:

1. **Technology**: The following are examples of programme technology, mainly systems, which you can develop or establish. Once they are in place and working well they contribute to your programme's efficiency and can help make your programme more sustainable.

Examples of Technology Sustainability:

- Development of your management styles and planning systems.
- A programme framework like social marketing or CBD.
- Training courses: On-the job and in-house capabilities.
- Use of local resources for providing expertise/ training.

II. **Behaviour**: Your programme has introduced a concept or intervention...such as selling and buying of condoms through kiosks, for **Example**...people have changed their behaviour to both sell and buy condoms in a kiosk, which was not previously the situation. As people continue to buy/sell condoms in kiosks, they have **sustained** a behaviour change because of your programme.

Examples of Behavioural Sustainability:

- The purchase of products, and no longer expecting free supply.
- Change in behaviour as a result of IE&C and BCC messages.
- The use of a product (condom), which was not a previous practice.

III. **Financial** Sustainability is understood, I think, by everyone. You can sell products (social marketing), services (IPPF clinics) and even the World Olympic Committee can generate revenues for financial sustainability by selling T-shirts, renting sports equipment, charging tickets to sporting events, etc.

	The next section of the handbook will cover
1	Ways to manage your programme towards sustainability.
2	Develop a triage for sustainability.
3	Planning for sustainability.

Sustainability Planning

We will not begin to cover the virtues of good planning, as everyone knows how important and necessary detailed planning...including strategic planning as covered in the previous sections of this handbook. Planning for sustainability of a programme will require more of your time, and certainly more detailed information, than some other components. Thinking about and planning for sustainability of a programme should **always** be included in your planning process, however, we don't believe it should be the driving force. In other words, you should **not** give up any undertaking - a good intervention or???... Just because it is not sustainable. Who is to say that it won't be sustainable later on?

Sustainability planning and things to look for

- Is cross subsidization possible - can costs, or common expenditures, be shared... In social marketing terms this could be having some costs of lower priced condoms covered by selling a premium brand or higher revenue generating products.

- Are subsidized or 'in-kind' commodities/equipment, including free office space, available from the government, other donors or NGOs. These items could be used in your programme for increased sustainability.
- Can other services (or components) of your programme help support your overall operations. In some reproductive health programmes the revenues from clinic operations or ultra sound services, help support the cost of other non-revenue generating Family Planning activities. These, purely income generating components can be a way to *sustain* your overall programme.
- Be creative in the breakdown of your expenses (costs) by putting them into the smallest components/items possible. By this, we mean be sure you itemize, or, consolidate, your budget expenditures by accurately allocating direct and/or indirect cost items.

An example: The cost of the photocopy machine could be included in one budget, but not in the other. Although the photocopy machine is used by both the projects, but only one has reflected the cost, thus making the second one more sustainable in terms of cost.

Other ways to appear more sustainable are:

1. Depreciate the cost of your vehicle over 'X' number of years thus reducing the annual project budget.
2. Proportion office space and equipment over several projects.
3. You have a training component that requires services of the head quarter's administrative person, a driver and two health service providers. In preparing the financial proposal, you could budget the head quarter's person and half of the driver's costs against the overhead and not as a direct project cost. This lowers the project budget and increases the sustainability aspects even more; ask your financial Manager how to do this.

- Always include an evaluation component, probably on a quarterly basis, in your proposals to monitor the progress (degree) of reaching your sustainability goal.

Also consider evaluations or monitoring systems that measure programme expenditures. Not only are reports on expenditures appreciated by donors, but they are generally a requirement. M&E (Monitoring/Evaluation) is a management tool that provides you, the person with the overall responsibility for the project, with good evidence based results for checking on sustainability, as well as identifying problems and checking on the status of any other achievements or failures.

How to support your sustainability planning?

Good sustainability planning begins with a good project design and proposal. These documents should have an M&E component, Financial Reporting Systems and an AUDIT plan.

Generally speaking, there should be monthly, or at a minimum, quarterly financial reports that cover expenditures and even measure expenditures against planned and projected budget allocations.

For programme achievements, a half-yearly Programme Report, covering targets, evidence based results and lessons learned should be prepared. Much of the material for the semi-annual report, as well as the annual or final report, will come from good M&E.

More detailed financial audits (internal and/or external), including inventory inspections, should be done on an annual basis. Most donors will tell you that the single most important (but not the only) factor for any organization seeking project funding is a proven record that it has the capability and systems to responsibly and timely receive, manage, and report the use of donor funds for mutually agreed on purposes.

Think Sustainable – Be Obtainable!

Sustainability through Triage

Triage is an important process, but a hard one to complete. The name *triage,* which is a term used in emergency medical procedures, is a situation where doctors determine which patients would get medical treatment (in order to survive) and in which order (priority) the treatment is given.

This section will cover what we call the 'triage' action, which simply means making a 'selection' of activities/components within a programme in order to survive...or in this case become more sustainable.

Triage can be seen as a necessary process in achieving programme sustainability. As the Manager, you must:

- ☑ Choose or select the way to make your programme sustainable. The *way* being, perhaps cutting activities, deselecting components, making changes in management design, reducing personnel or ???
- ☑ Choose or select what steps to take to make your programme sustainable. The *steps* perhaps being reducing procurement costs, providing less external training, or charging higher fees for certain services or ???
- ☑ Choose or select what components can be sustainable; outreach programmes, specific products, IE&C materials development or???
- ☑ Choose or select the areas – technological and financial which you want to make sustainable.

What Can You Expect to Achieve from Triage?

There are several features of 'triage'. From your efforts, you can expect to receive several benefits. A few are listed below:

- Triage is, in some respects, a more critical exercise and takes a harder look at a programme, than; say a mid-term review (MTR) or an evaluation. Triage can provide you with a very good baseline for your programme. In the triage process you and your staff not only look at the activities and related components (financial, use of consultants, available resources), but you also look at everything from the context of how do I make it better (improve or fix it), and/or how do I eliminate it and carry on without it. An evaluation is more of an assessment...triage is more of a re-design with the cut and change results. Your benefit is that now you really have a thorough understanding of your programme.

- Triage gives you an opportunity to make decisions and prioritise not only your activities, but also your implementation steps. In addition, the triage process affords you the chance of redefining your complete operational programme approach, including goals and objectives, so that they can be more sustainable. Your benefit here is, because you now have a roadmap you can make some hard decisions, and make your programme more sustainable.

Steps to Complete a Triage:

Exercise

On separate sheets of paper write down each of the following for your current ongoing total programme (i.e., ALL project goals on one piece of paper, on another piece of paper show ALL the resources -combined, not by individual project or sub-project).

1. Goals (primary and secondary) for all projects.
2. Resources (and from where they come domestic/ foreign).
3. Objectives (long and short term) for all projects.
4. Overhead/operations personnel (all, including guards, drivers).
5. Direct project personnel (all full and part time).
6. Components of the project (broadly stated...training, health provision).
7. Activities of all the projects be specific here, management training, etc.
8. Total project budget, not by line item, just total funds available...one figure.

Let's assume you have been told that you have only 40% of the total budget for this year (point 8 shown above), and that there are only 6.5 months to complete the total programme. Now take all the components (point 6 above) ditto earlier comment and prioritise them, not in order of importance, but in the order in which components can be completed in 6.5 months, likewise, with the activities. Now identify the personnel needed to implement/manage the activities/components, plus the resources (remember you only have 6.5 months to complete the project). Finally set your goals and objectives. What were you able to achieve and what parts are or can be sustainable? What part is not sustainable? What did you learn? What are the next steps forward? How would you approach the programme now? What would you do if additional funding were to be made available, and how would you proceed?

As is always the case in management...there are no right or wrong answers! This exercise is best completed individually and then discussed as a group, where brainstorming is the call of the day.

Using Management Tools for Improved Sustainability:

Of prime importance is the part dealing with the **financial management** tool, or financial creativity, as we say in some cases. Sustainability, any aspect of it, will involve or be influenced by finances. Like the old saying goes "money talks or nobody walks." And finances can be defined here as revenues, income, profit, cost recovery, subsidy, lines of credit, grants, loans, taxes and certainly debts.

Management of your programme is something that you, as the Manager/Director do every day, including managing your programme *towards* sustainability. You probably do this without even thinking about it, or realising that you are doing so.

All management tools, from goal setting to time management, influence your programme's sustainability...or lack of sustainability. If the tools are applied, and when they are used well, you can increase your chances of being sustainable.

Knowledge Required:

As a rule of thumb for managing your programme towards sustainability, each Manager/Director should have a very clear understanding of the following:

- Extensive knowledge of your clients, target group/audience, and beneficiaries. The more you know about the people you are assisting or targeting, the better you will be able to sustain your programme. Remember the programme is being implemented basically to serve/cater to this group.
- Know and recognise the most expensive sections/departments/components of your programme. Most likely, it is these expensive items that will hold you back from reaching higher levels of sustainability, and they need to be monitored carefully and regularly. You might not be able to change the situation, but, at least you have pinpointed where the money is being spent, and how much is being allocated.

- A thorough knowledge of your resources, both financial and human. List them down, analyse them and prepare plans to properly utilise what is available to you. Which of the resources can you do without, reduce or limit? Good management of resources, with the right amount of financial management, is one key to sustainability.

Where to start?

To start we need to go back to the beginning of this section–approaching sustainability and take a look at the three areas once again–technology, behaviour and financial. It is a common belief that some programmes can and do reach sustainability, albeit at varying levels. What has assisted the Managers in reaching this *level* of sustainability can be directly related to the management tools that s/he has used in project planning and implementation. The following will serve as a guide to what management tools can be applied to different areas of sustainability.

Some Great Management Tools

The **management tools** to apply for improved sustainability include:

For Technology

- Goal Setting... Clearer goals and smarter objectives will define the aim of your programme better and reduce costs.
- Planning and Organization...will strengthen the programme implementation, reducing costs (travel, communication) and provide more efficient resource utilisation.
- Communications... To improve overall implementation and enhance behaviour change.
- Supervision... Ensuring the programme principle and designs are followed and the framework is effectively utilised for programme inputs.

- Time Management... Also included in financial sustainability, will support the effective implementation of the programme.

For Behaviour

1. Financial Systems... That includes the development and design of procurement, tendering and credit systems for all components of the programme.
2. Performance Appraisals...including Human Resource development/training.
3. Motivation and Team Working...For capacity building that will strengthen programme implementation and assist reaching sustainability as outlined in #2 under technology.

For Financial Sustainability

☑ Audit Reviews...Look at resource allocations as well as system efficiency.

☑ Financial Reporting...Indicates fiscal management efficiency and where levels of sustainability can be reached/maintained.

☑ Logistics Management...Especially true for social marketing or outreach programmes.

☑ Strategic Planning...Incorporates all aspects of the programme; planning, goal setting, design, budgeting into one planning picture.

☑ Time Management...Time is money, and thus in order to reach any level of sustainability you will have to complete the work in a timely fashion and in the most efficient manner.

A management tool that has impact on all the three areas of sustainability is **monitoring and evaluation**. This is self-explanatory, and I believe everyone can see where the application of this management tool will affect, positively, their programme efficiency and assist in reaching higher levels of sustainability.

2.2.8. Time Management

Time is something that once lost can never be retrieved...Regardless of your wealth or status in life.

Overview

In other sections of this handbook, we have covered and discussed some elements of Time Management. In this section, however we will cover Time Management in complete detail. **Remember:** Do not waste your time... And do not let someone or something rob you of your time.

Techniques and Insight on How to Make More Time Available:

Isn't that really the idea of time management (and the need of most Managers and Directors) – to make more time available. Don't we try to put more productive hours in the workday.

Hopefully the following paragraphs will help you to use time more effectively! And a good place to start is by asking yourself the question: Do you manage your time or does your time manage you? Ask yourself this question and then think about it.

Success in Time Management

To be Successful in Time Management you will have to:
• Make some changes in your work patterns/schedules.
• Accept to do certain new things, like keep a time log.
• Learn how to prioritise.
• Develop and follow an action plan.
• Learn and express a willingness to delegate tasks.
• Identify (and eliminate) time wasters.
• Learn relaxing techniques.

Let's start by identifying the **broad functions** that you as the Manager/Director spend time performing. Knowing and identifying the task that you must perform is the first step...The second is then allocating an amount of *time* to complete the task.

An example:

One broad function is planning. By detailing what all goes into planning (preparing budgets, setting goals, etc.) you are also now in a position to determine the amount of time that will be required to complete these tasks...plus who should do them and by what time (deadline).

Here are four major broad functions:

1. Planning (long and short term)
2. Organising and staffing
3. Coordinating and Directing
4. Controlling (supervising)

Now from the four (4) broad functions above you must then:

- Prioritise the functions, starting with the function where you spend the most time.
- Then identify which of these functions you could perhaps delegate to others -in part or whole.
- By looking at the above functions, and your prioritised list, can you now identify where time is wasted (continually preparing planning documents that duplicate other documents, to many staff meetings to discuss the function, or poorly designed lines of coordination).

By completing the above, it is now possible to make a **Personal Time Profile**. When answering the above questions it is best to write your answers on a piece of paper and put them in a chart or table format, as described below.

Personal Time Profile

Good time management really starts with yourself...After all it's **your** time that you are trying to manage more effectively. Of course, good time management on your part will also have spin-off effects on your team/group and the organisation's overall performance.

In the paragraphs above, we spoke of a personal time profile. To develop a time profile, we start by making a chart, illustrated below, and get into what we call **taking a closer look at ourselves.**

The time profile is based on the four broad functions indicated above and consists of the following steps:

- ☑ Review the four broad functions (planning, etc.).
- ☑ Prioritize the functions in a descending order (most important to least important).
- ☑ Identify which functions can be delegated (a major time saver).
- ☑ Identify the time wasters, and/or where there is duplication of efforts, etc.

The personal time profile can be daily/weekly/monthly. Anything longer than a month isn't practical. The chart is simple, and not only sets out a time table for you, but also acts as a planning and monitoring table for your staff and their time usage as well. The five (5) headings are standard; regardless it is a daily/weekly/monthly profile.

Let's look at this illustrative example:

Name/type of activity or task to complete or be undertaken	**What action is to be taken or carried out**	**The action is to be completed or taken by whom**	**When and how much TIME is allocated to complete the task**	**Remarks and/or special instructio ns**
Example: Airport pick up of the new representati ve at Otepeni airport	Pick up new representative and take her and her family to Hotel Hilton on Isai boulevard	Office driver Tomescu using blue 4 X 4 jeep, take Marious with you	Malev flt. #12 arrives 19 Feb. at 1100 hrs from Budapest. Go directly to hotel and report back to office by 1300	Take signboar d with you, Lei 100,000 in currency and city map.

Can you see where the Manager/Director has saved his/her time by preparing this profile? Can you list three ways where time was saved? Can you see other advantages of good management when such a profile/chart is prepared? (Hint: Please note the clear instructions to driver, thus eliminating any confusion or the need to **come back** to the Manager/Director to ask additional questions…another major time saver. If you can get the message across by saying it only once you have saved many minutes of your time (and frustration as well).

Task Oriented Time Profile

Given below is another sample of a time profile, which is very task and time specific. Note even the calendar date is included plus the estimated time to complete the task. This chart is completed/prepared by the driver (from the above example), and not the Manager. Another good (time) management exercise is for the Manager or the employee to review the chart after completing the task and check to see exactly how long did it take as compared to the estimated time. The benefit here might be finding a more efficient way of doing the task, better planning or a way to save time.

TASK/ACTION	BY WHOM	TIME
Wash/clean the jeep.	Office cleaner	18/2 after 1500 hrs…1 hr
Get money for petrol from cashier.	Self (Tomescu)	18/2 while jeep being cleaned…30 minutes
Call airlines' confirm flight is on time.	Secretary	19/2 at 0900 …10 minutes
Depart from the office at 1030 hrs depart for airport.	Self along with Marious	19/2 drop off and return to office by 1300… 2 ½ hrs

Without this profile, the Manager might possibly think that the airport pick up should take about two hours. S/he did not consider the amount of time needed to prepare for the pick-up, the staff involved other than the driver and that s/he might be without the use of the jeep for up to four hours. This is a good planning and time management chart, all wrapped up into one management tool.

Looking at Ourselves

You can fool some of the people some of the time, but...We believe you can't fool yourself. Therefore, it's always good to take a 'close' look at ourselves and examine our actions. The following questions are designed to do just that; in addition to help form an analysis of how you might better utilise your time.

Exercise

The first set of questions is for Managers/Directors only, the second set is for employees and the third and fourth set for both to answer.

How often have you heard yourself saying (pick one answer only): –

1) I wouldn't have these time management problems if only my employees would:

___ Work faster.

___ Do what I tell them.

___ Stop asking so many questions.

___ Be more motivated.

___ Learn to write better.

___ Stay off the phone.

___ Stop sending/reading so many jokes over the e-mail.

___ Other____________________ (your criticism here).

2) I would not have time management problems if my Manager/Director would only:

___ Leave me alone.

___ Tell me what s/he expects.

___ Give me reasonable work.

___ Learn to delegate better.

___ Assign me a job and let me do it.

___ Let me have an assistant.

___ Schedule fewer meetings.

___ Other____________________ (your criticism here).

3) I would not have these time management problems if my family would only:

___ Be more considerate of me.

___ Stop doing all these *things*.

___ Give me some time for myself.

___ Tell me what they expect from me.

___ Stop signing me up for activities I am not interested in.

___ Learn to read my mind.

___ Other____________________ (your criticism here).

4) How many times have you said, 'I would not have these time management problems' if:

___ We didn't have these unnecessary rules.

___ This company could get itself organized.

___ The telephone would stop ringing... Just for a day.

___ I didn't have all these meetings to go to.

___ People would stop asking me to do so much.

___ Other________________________ (your criticism here).

Now that we know a little more about ourselves, in the next section we will begin to take a look at what consumes our time...and perhaps what wastes our time as well. Identifying time wasters is a key to good time management.

Improving Time Usage

All of us have the **opportunity** to improve the usage of our personal time. And we all have experienced time related problems in our job. The secret is to turn these problems into opportunities. To do this I think we have to understand the reason for the problems.

The next two sections will cover: (1) Some ways to improve your time use; and (2) Identifying time wasters or time consumers. I'm not sure which one you may wish to present to your staff first, but from our perspective we always like to understand the reason for the problems (of wasting time) before moving forward, but it is really up to you.

In the following chart the problems (shown as items) are given, and you, as an individual must then rank the severity of the problem as it relates to your goal of improving time usage. To complete this exercise simply read the item and then rank the severity of the problem by putting an 'X' in the box you feel best ranks the problem. Once you know the problem areas then you can begin to take steps to solve them. This chart will help you focus in on what problem areas waste your time.

Exercise

S. No.	Item	Strongly Agree	Slightly Agree	Strongly Disagree	Slightly Disagree
1.	Other people always seem to come to me for advice.				
2.	My work tends to pile up.				
3.	I never seem to have time to myself.				
4.	I spend too much time in meetings.				
5.	I always seem to be trying to do too many things at the same time.				
6.	I tend to put off unpleasant jobs.				

7.	I tend to lose or misplace document/ memos.				
8.	I never have time to think.				
9.	The telephone never seems to stop ringing.				
10.	I am always writing letters, memos, reports.				
11.	I spend too much time travelling from place to place.				
12.	I have to start and stop jobs frequently				
13.	I have to spend a lot of time answering or sending e-mails.				
14.	I find it difficult to say 'no' to the requests of other people.				

Now you know the problem areas… But how are you going to solve them? The solution(s) can be worked out individually or with the help and support of your Manager/Director or even your group/team members.

It is advisable that you set goals, with a time limit of course, on how you are going to try and solve the problem(s). What problems do you think you should start with first…The ones that only consume your time slightly, the ones that consume most of your time (biggest problem), ones that are most easy to solve or ... For the answers, continue reading the next section.

Some Answers to your Time Solving Questions:

So far we have looked at ways to make more time available (by better planning, delegation); at preparing time profiles (prioritising tasks) analysing our time (activities/schedules) and finally trying to solve the time consuming problems to improve our time usage. So, what are you doing with all this FREE time you have now… If you are smart you won't tell anybody and just relax.

But before you fall asleep, let's discuss two more time management points. The first will look at what we call the all time consumers…Meaning they waste your time every (all the) time, and not just occasionally. The second is a wrap up overview of ideas to help you understand better, the time management in general.

The best way to tackle the time problem is, whatever way is best, most convenient, and feasible for you.

'All time' time consumers

What wastes your time? Please tick (x) those that affect **you** most often…Then if you have time, you can rank them in order of the most frequent.

	poor listening habits		too much information
	too much talking		misinformation
	inappropriate conversation		inconsiderate co-workers
	doing instead of managing		failure to set priorities
	difficulty in delegating		failure to get feedback
	involving people who aren't "involved"		crisis management
	failure to find the real problem		telephone conversations
	Premature decision making		poor written communications
	blame; fault finding		meetings
	jumping to conclusions		lack of agendas
	Fear		failure to follow agendas
	Time estimates too short		fatigue

	Time estimates too long		e-mail
	poor planning		no policy on routine matters
	no planning		lack of proper equipment
	poor organisation		outdated procedures
	overlapping of responsibilities		low motivation
	Can't say *no*		not knowing what is wanted
	failure to think things through		doing everything myself
	putting it off-procrastination		lack of daily plan
	doing too many things at once		confusing chain of command
	same paper work over and over again		unclear expectations

Some Important Ideas about Time Management

These concepts and principles of time management should be explained to your team/group and understood by all.

- ☑ Analyse Your Time Use Patterns: Keep a daily/weekly time log of your activities...This is essential for effective time management.
- ☑ Always Anticipate: Expect the unexpected and plan for it... Even simple things like sufficient supply of pens/paper to an extra pair of eyeglasses kept in your office or in your brief case.
- ☑ Always Plan: Every hour spent in effective planning saves three hours in execution... Planning is both long range and daily... Don't be afraid (embarrassed) to write things down...make to-do lists.
- ☑ Be Flexible: Flexibility in scheduling time may be necessary because of things that are beyond your control.
- ☑ Set Objectives and Priorities: Most effective RESULTS are achieved through well thought out and planned objectives. Prioritise your tasks, don't waste time on less important tasks... Planning will help keep this from happening.
- ☑ I mpose Deadlines: Exercising self-discipline; imposing deadlines and sticking to them, will help you overcome indecision and procrastination.

- ☑ Consolidate Activities: Similar tasks should be grouped within time divisions (in the afternoon or certain hours) of the work day...example: Receive visitors only between 1000 hrs and 1200 hrs.
- ☑ Concentrate Effort: A few critical actions (about 20% of your actions) generally produce the majority of the work... Therefore, you should concentrate your efforts on these few actions.
- ☑ Aim for Effectiveness: Effectiveness is doing the right job right!... Your effort, no matter how efficient, will be ineffective if performed on the wrong tasks.
- ☑ Delegate: Tasks, decision-making should be delegated... Remember the three key points of proper delegation... You should avoid having the staff becoming dependent on you.
- ☑ Minimize Routine Work and Avoid Detail: Routine tasks of low value (importance) to your overall objectives should be minimized, consolidated or delegated...deal/work with essential information only.
- ☑ Control Paperwork : High stacks of paper on your desk is not a sign that you are indispensable... Deal with paperwork immediately and handle each piece of paper only once... Make use of the waste paper basket, make notations on incoming documents and return immediately...route some reports to others.
- ☑ Failure to Follow-up on actions: (My own or those under my supervision) can consume a lot of time in picking up after failed or lagging actions—even though, up front, it might seem like a waste of time.

2.2.9. Management by Objectives (MBO)

Simply stated in the MBO system you establish your objectives...What you want to achieve, and then manage your resources to reach those objectives

Overview

A form of management, very popular in the 1970's and 1980's, was Management by Objectives (MBO). Starting in the 1990's the MBO format was replaced, in many organizations, by Results Based Management (RBM). Donors in particular were more concerned about achieving *results* from the funds they were providing than only knowing what objectives you *hoped* to achieve.

However, the principles and many facets of MBO are still used today by many planners/Managers and we thought it would be good to include a brief background of both. In the MBO system, you establish your objectives...what you want to achieve, and then manage your resources to reach those objectives.

THE MBO SYSTEM

The MBO is a system in which:

- Objectives are set jointly.
- Objectives are set prior to implementation.
- Performance can be measured.

To introduce and complete an MBO you should:

- Determine what needs to be done to reach your objective.
- Determine if objectives relate to overall objectives of the organization.
- Determine time limits (set a time frame).
- Evaluate your MBO activities when completed.

When using the MBO system you will:

- Improve your own management style and increase the efficiency of the organization.
- You can build a better team, because you jointly decide on an action to be taken/followed.
- You can utilize resources better, both human and financial, because you know what direction you are headed; and
- You can better monitor/appraise the quality of the work undertaken.

During the MBO process the boss (Manager/Director) is either monitoring and/or measuring the **performance.** (Note: In RBM you monitor indicators to see evidence of **results**). Once you have reached your objective(s) it is then time to evaluate the process and outcomes. A good Manager always wants to improve and do better... Evaluating the work done is a good first step.

Evaluating your MBO:

Along with your staff, undertake the following evaluation. Be sure to record the responses and don't be afraid to be critical of your actions... We learn from doing!

- ☑ Review your accomplishments.
- ☑ Consider if the tasks/activities achieved are in line with the set objectives (yes/no).

Ask yourself:

- ☑ Could you have found alternative ways to achieve your objectives?
- ☑ Was more research necessary?
- ☑ Did you need more training in order to reach the objectives?
- ☑ Did you have enough resources...money, people, equipment?
- ☑ Other comments/observations.

An MBO requires the setting of objectives and well-trained, motivated people to implement an MBO. In an MBO system, the programme sets objectives to be achieved, and likewise, the Manager also sets objectives for the staff/team. Below is a list of what a Manager should consider when evaluating the personnel implementing an MBO programme.

Some Comments and Points to Remember:

- ☑ To accomplish his/her objectives a Manager manages people.
- ☑ To the extent possible, you should state the objectives in terms of measurable results.

- ☑ It is usually advantageous for the boss to set the creative goal of a position.
- ☑ Your objectives should encourage some improvement in your performance.
- ☑ Your objectives should be in writing and agreed to by boss/subordinate.
- ☑ Objectives should change.
- ☑ Objectives apply to the person; therefore, objectives for a new person should be set in light of his/her experience.
- ☑ Objectives should be set for a person in areas where s/he has influence over the results.
- ☑ The prime value of an objective is in the stimulation of a person.
- ☑ If objectives are to stimulate the person then, s/he must feel the objectives are fair.

Establishing a Time Frame:

A big part of the MBO is identifying steps to reach the objective, establishing a time frame for achieving the steps, and ultimately reaching the final objective. This same time frame chart, shown below can be used to monitor and measure the progress in achieving the objective. The time frame chart should be prepared by the subordinate and then reviewed, and discussed with the Manager/Director.

An example:

The objective of the Family Planning Association of Armenia was to introduce the injectable contraceptive "Depo Provera" into their family planning programme. We have started to prepare their time frame chart... Can you think of additional steps to fill in the blanks?

STEPS TO ACCOMPLISH OBJECTIVE	BEGINNING DATE	ENDING DATE
1. Market research on Depo Provera	01 Feb. 2002	28 Feb. 2002

2. Analysis data	03 Mar. 2002	04 Mar. 2002
3.		
4.		
LIST OF MATERIALS NEEDED		
1. VEHICLE	01 Feb. 2002	28 Feb. 2002
2.		
COORDINATION & ASSISTANCE NEEDED		
1. Research assistant (x2)	01 Feb. 2002	28 Feb. 2002
2. Data Analysis person	05 Feb. 2002	20 Feb. 2002
3.		
FINANCIAL NEEDS		
1. Petrol costs	$100 per week starting 01 Feb. 2002	21 Feb. 2002
2. per diem (x3)	$20/week starting 01 Feb. 2002	28 February 2002
3.		
Obstacles/Barriers		
1. No money		
2. Respective. personnel not available		
3.		

Another example:

Given below is another possible 'time line' to be considered. In this time line, basically, the activities are shown in the vertical column, and scheduled for completion in a specified time period (week/month/quarter, etc.), which is shown horizontally. Some Managers find this table easier to read/monitor.

Activity Time Line

Activity/Time	Month 1	Month 2	Month 3	Month 4	Month 5	Month 6
Sign Contract						
Mobilize Staff						
Set-up Office						
Conduct Research						
Workshop						
Final Report						

2.2.10. Results Based Management (RBM)

- Results Based Management (RBM) provides a coherent framework for strategic planning and management based on accountability and lessons learned.
- RBM aims to improve management effectiveness and accountability by defining realistic and expected results.

Overview

The process of Results Based Management (RBM) is fairly new, not totally understood and certainly not appreciated by everybody yet. USAID, The EU, The World Bank and UN organizations are suggesting that RBM be used, tried and applied when preparing project proposals. There are aspects of the RBM that can greatly assist programme implementation, and introducing those features in this section is our goal.

We believe that the process of RBM begins with problem identification. After that, MBO principles should be applied, especially in setting realistic objectives, followed by the ability to record change (with evidence) as a result of the project/programme intervention.

The four basic pillars in RBM are:

1. Definition of strategic goals, which provide a focus for action.
2. Specification of expected results.
3. Ongoing monitoring and assessment of performance.
4. Improved accountability based on continuous feedback.

Features of RBM Approach

The main feature of RBM is the focus on measuring the RESULTS achieved by the project's action/activities. Even if the outcome may be lower (less) than the planned objectives, the measurement of the results still indicates what has actually been produced during implementation. Perhaps this simple illustration given below will help explain.

Results are: Outputs and Outcomes. The result of an *output* is the *outcome* of the activity. In the illustration below you will note that when people are trained (output) the outcome of the training is new jobs created. The evidence of the training is increased income of the people.

Inputs	Outputs	lead to	Outcomes	Impact
Experts, Equipment, Funds	People Trained, Courses Completed	>>>>	Jobs Created, Income Increased	Improved Health, Longer Life

By examining the results, you can show the level of change and the impact. This level of change can form the basis/baseline for the next phase of project, including identification of steps necessary for reaching sustainability. A good way to measure the level of change is through quantitative and qualitative research.

Another important feature in RBM is the use of indicators to show *proof* of results. Because RBM approach looks at the results, and the level of change, greater emphasis is placed on the use of indicators and more attention is paid to measuring outcomes than previously practiced. Therefore, data collection will also become critical in the application of RBM.

The following paragraphs will provide a detailed background on RBM, its application and show its strengths as a project/programme management instrument.

Understanding the Differences and Strengths of MBO and RBM:

DIFFERENCES	
MBO	RBM
Measures performance. Focus is on setting objectives. Details how to achieve objectives. More of a monitoring process. More development oriented.	Measures change. Focus is achieving results. Details on proof of results. More an evaluation process. More business-like approach.
STRENGTHS	
Builds a good working team. Provides long term planning process. Develops staff/personnel.	Provides stakeholder mgt. Shows action/change quickly Builds good partners. Identifies sustainability issues.

Review with your programme Managers/staff, the differences and strengths of the MBO and RBM listed in the table above. After reviewing, try to determine if there should be a change or shift in your programme operations.

Problem Identification using RBM

In order for the RBM to be useful, the Manager/Director must be able to identify the problems correctly and describe them clearly. Problem Identification is the first step in preparing a RBM approach and is as critical, if not more so, than the setting of objectives in an MBO. After the problem is identified, then like in the MBO, programme objectives and goals are set and activities listed.

It is at this point, where the difference between MBO and RBM begins. In MBO the setting/identification of **objectives** is the main focus and, all the energies and resources of the project are directed towards achieving the objectives. In RBM it is the results, not the objectives...That are measured and evaluated. The actions taken/implemented in RBM approach are for producing results, supported by evidence, with the project's achievement determined by these verifiable results.

What is interesting in RBM approach is that the results, which are verified by indicators, can be lower than the set objectives. Also the *level* of results can be used as the basis for negotiating/designing the next phase of the project.

Steps in Preparing a RBM Approach

Be sure to follow and include the following **steps** in your proposal:

6-Basis for Sustainability

5-Expected Result (level of change)

4-Identification of Indicators (for proof of results)

3-Listing of Activities (who, what resources needed)

2-Setting of Goals and Objectives (realistic and achievable)

1-Problem Identification (clear and concise)

Exercise

Following the steps to problem identification, using RBM, (see above), now set realistic and achievable goals, and objectives. Like the MBO, the setting of goals and objectives can be done jointly with the Manager/Director and the staff/team member. After setting the goals and objectives, prepare a list of activities (actions) to be carried out.

Getting the Results!

The MBO and RBM process have been, somewhat, similar up to this point. However, at this stage in RBM we begin to look at and measure the **results (expected results)** of the project. In the RBM, *results* are measured by indicators, which reveal *proof* of the *results,* or impact. Potential indicators in an RBM could be: (1) the baseline (2) effect (result of the outputs) and (3) impact.

Example:

A simple RBM programme planning example prepared for a social marketing programme:

Male latex condoms (input) are included in BCC campaigns (output) implemented through social marketing programmes (process). This leads to increased use of male condoms (effect) that reduces the incidence of STIs/STDs (impact) noted in the MoH prevalence rates (baseline). The last three (3) indicators are most suitable for the RBM.

NOTE: In MBO at this stage, you would be looking at objectives and measuring programme performance (not results).

Simply put, the results are the outcome of the actions. The results are measured by indicators. Results also bring about a certain level of change. This level of change, with respect to the programme objectives, should also be measured. Quantitative and qualitative research is a good way to measure this change.

It is important to note that the results achieved can be lower than the set programme objectives. The results can also be shown in percentage and used to establish a firm baseline for the next phase, or project. This is true because you have already achieved *a level of* results.

The **important link** here, especially for donors, is:

- That you have achieved some results.
- Measured them by using solid indicators.
- Verified them.
- Have thus established a basis for sustainability.

Exercise

In the section, 'features of RBM' (page 103) you were asked to prepare a list of activities. Assuming that you completed at least one of the activities, this exercise will ask you to identify two indicators that you would use to measure the results, and set up a research ToR for measuring the level of change. (Hint: See results above).

2.2.11. Performance Appraisals

Performance Appraisals
Personnel Evaluations
Training Needs Analysis
Job Descriptions
Competencies

General comment

For the purpose of this handbook, the structure and comments provided on performance appraisals (PAs) operate under the assumption that the Manager/Director will be reviewing the employee as an individual.

However, the Manager/Director must keep in mind a common dilemma of an individual's performance in a strong *team environment*. On one hand, the PA is written as a document for an individual, often a striving individual who is like most climbing the ladder to success as an achieving individual.

On the other hand, the organization may be speaking *think team* in its management guidance and giving high marks (at least in meetings) to collaborative team behaviour. An employee can get caught unfairly in middle...Between doing for him/herself or *differing* self to the team. It's rather like the football/soccer player who has the option of shooting for the goal himself or passing to another striker and letting him try for the goal.

Overview

Performance Appraisal (PA) is a key management tool, but one that I fear is often neglected or only implemented in part. We view Performance Appraisal as an instrument that will:

1. Assist the Manager/Director in identifying training needs.
2. Objectively, set a basis for pay increases/bonuses.
3. Motivate, build capacity and improve skills and;
4. Determine future personnel actions–positive and negative.

The Performance Appraisal is also called, or known, by many other names: Personnel Evaluations or Personnel Evaluation Reviews are a couple of the most common names used, and may account for some of the confusion.

Preparing a Performance Appraisal:

Performance Appraisals go beyond just an *evaluation*. The Performance Appraisal material covered in this section will include four key areas:

Key Areas of a Performance Appraisal
a. Job Descriptions b. Competency Profiles c. Training Needs Analysis d. Development of a Performance Appraisal Policy

This section could include other aspects on performance appraisals, like performance appraisal formats or performance communications. However PA formats/designs are often dictated or designed by the organization…As there are, to some extent in-house PA policies. So, these topics are not covered in great detail in this handbook. For the moment, we will concentrate only on points (a) to (d) above, starting with job descriptions.

Job Descriptions

Job Descriptions should be prepared for everyone, including the Director. Job Descriptions should be clear and concise…Use as many words as you need to describe the job/tasks accurately. You should prepare a Job Description to avoid hearing words like "you never told me that" or" I didn't know that was a part of my job."

The main goal of a Job Description is to avoid the employer-employee friction that takes up so much management time as well as creating an unpleasant atmosphere in the office. It's a good idea to review/discuss Job Descriptions during interviews with prospective/new employees, and when there is a position change (promotion/demotion) involving an existing staff member.

Job Descriptions should be prepared in compliance and written within the *law of the land*. The Job Description must be signed by both the employer and employee, and attached to the employment contract. The Job Description usually goes with the position (not the individual), but the Job Description should clearly state what qualifications are required by the individual to do the Job. Like most management tools, the Job Description should be reviewed regularly, revised as needed and adjusted to the local terms and conditions.

The Job Description, which can also describe responsibilities that go with the position, focuses on:

- ☑ Input
- ☑ Behaviour
- ☑ Structure

When preparing the Job Description, you may also wish to include a few lines that point out the responsibilities involved in the position...including things like authority, coordination, etc.

An example:

1. The Team member administers/manages 'X'...and reports to 'Y'.
2. The Team member maintains 'X' (equipment/logs, etc.)...
3. The Team member is authorized to 'X' (sign checks, use vehicle, etc.)
4. The Team member is responsible for organizing 'X' (workshops, etc.)

5. The Team member coordinates 'X' (official meetings/ visitors).

Sample Job Description Form:

After reviewing the following sample...and reflecting on your own staff/team what changes would you like to make to this form?

1. Job Title:
2. Qualification: (To include formal education and work experience)
3. Scale of Salary: (Range of salary – starting/ending salary)
4. Supervisor/Report to: (Also how often, how (written, verbally or??)
5. Responsible to:
6. Job Location: (Indicate travel if necessary, possible location change)
7. Main purpose of job: (Purpose, not what s/he will be doing)
8. Duties: (These should be very well detailed in order of priority)
9. Working Conditions: (Time/hours, location, inside/outside office, knowledge of equipment (computers/special software, etc.)
10. Social Condition: (Who does s/he work with...is there public contact-salesman or speaker, fund raiser, etc.)
11. Promotion Prospect: (Promotion after what length of service, to what position, what additional qualifications/experience is needed, etc.)
12. Remarks:

Competency

In the section above, we discussed the *Job Description*, which is an instrument that **describes** the job or position, along with a list of other personal/job requirements. A good compliment to the Job

Description and again, something that is not very frequently', used, is a *Competency Profile,* which explains what attributes the employee is **expected** to have or to achieve in order to be considered for a certain job/position. The competency profile should identify and/or outline what is *essential* for the person/employee to have, in order to perform successfully in this position.

(Note: It is recognized that everybody may not have all the attributes essential to fill the position, (thus training is a part of Performance Appraisals), but the competency profile does represent what is ideal for this position.

Attributes Included in a Competency Profile

The Manager/Director must decide the attributes, which are critical or most relevant/essential for the position. The required attributes may change from position to position...Again recognizing it's not a perfect world and that one person may not have all the essential attributes. Included in the list are:

1. Knowledge (formal, practical, local culture/conditions)
2. Skills (technical, inter-personal, communication)
3. Values (honesty, ethical)
4. Attitudes (positive, creative, willingness to learn)
5. Behaviours (negative, positive, cooperative)
6. Traits (self-control, patience, hard working)

Using a Competency Profile

- Recruitment or Placement: The competency profile can be discussed during job interviews, along with the Job Description, and can assist in evaluating different qualities between candidates by ranking/totalling the number of attributes each employee has.
- Setting Performance Standards: Existing employees always (usually) want to move *up the ladder* within an organization. The posting of competency profiles for each position can be

a way to inform the employee what s/he is expected to attain in order to be considered for this higher position.

- Performance Feedback and Development: The competency profile provides a framework for individual self-assessment or receiving feedback from the Manager/Director.

Exercise

Select a vacant position you wish to fill and identify the attributes and competencies essential to perform successfully in this position.

Hint: The list above can help, but try to expand on the above. Example: Systematic thinking (judgement, conceptualization).

Training Needs Analysis

In the following paragraphs we will discuss "Training Needs Analysis"...and NOT Training Needs Assessment... Did you notice the difference? The distinction is made between the two because we believe many Managers/Directors try to asses the training needs before fully understanding (analyze) the job/employment **situation** and/or the **ability** of the employee. A Training Needs Assessment should **follow** the Training Needs analysis. Without a good Training Needs Analysis, an organization can waste a lot of money in providing the wrong training.

Example:

Because there has been a reporting change, within the organization, the senior clerk's position now requires knowledge in higher-level mathematics. The Manager/Director reacts automatically and immediately arranges for the senior clerk to have training in higher mathematics. However, the person holding the clerk's position is poor in advanced higher mathematics, and s/he has never done well in any math subject. Moreover s/he doesn't like math.

By jumping to the conclusion that the employee needs *training in math*, without doing an analysis (looking at the situation and/or the employee's ability) will result in several problems. The organization will spend (waste) a large amount of money on *training* an employee who doesn't want to learn the new math skills and who, perhaps, doesn't have the ability to learn them anyway. In addition, the employee cannot perform well and is unhappy, office morale goes down, the organization isn't reaching its goals because the clerk isn't doing his/her job correctly, and the Manager has extra work because of the many mistakes made by the clerk.

What to do?

The key is to link the **position** (situation) to the employee's **ability** and **likes** (desires). In a **Training Needs Analysis,** the first step is to take a good look at the actual job/position, including what is actually required to do the job. What the demands are (physical and/or mental), the expected standards, and performance levels to be achieved. Required skills (management, language, inter-personal) and even something as simple as being able to drive a car, can be a part of the analysis.

Some other characteristics to consider include age, years of experience, health, ability to travel, even identification of the person's weaknesses. The detailed Job Description you prepare will help analyze the job/position clearly and support your analysis.

Likewise, the Competency Profile will spell out the required attributes (knowledge, traits), which can be tested to confirm the employee's ability. Once the situation and employee's ability is clarified then any shortfall in the required skill level can be addressed by providing training.

Questionnaires can help!

The Manager/Director will make an analysis of the situation from his/her perspective, but it's also a good idea to get the employee involved in the Training Needs Analysis. The following page offers some suggested questions, an employee can respond to, and should be considered in the analysis.

Employee's Self Analysis Questionnaire

Instructions: Please answer each question to show how you feel. You may circle the response that describes your *own* feeling the best. The only correct answer is your frank opinion.

1. Think about the specific duties of your job. How often have you felt unable to use your full capabilities in the performance of your job?

Almost Always	Very Often	Fairly Often	Not Very Often	Very Seldom	Almost Never

2. As you see it, how many opportunities do you feel you have in your job for making worthwhile contributions?

Almost None	Very Few	A Few	Quite a Few	A Great Many	Unlimited

3. If additional training is provided, are the opportunities increased?

Yes	No	Explain

4. How frequently have you felt in your job that you could accomplish more, if you could have complete freedom of action to accomplish your objectives?

Almost All The Time	Most of The Time	Quite Often	Not Too Often	Very Seldom	Almost Never

5. How do you feel about your present assignment as a job where you can continually learn?

Nothing More To Learn On It	Practically Nothing to Learn	Can Learn Something But Not Much	Still Can Learn a Little	Can Still Learn a Lot On It	Can Still Learn a Great Deal

6. To what extent is it possible to know whether you are doing well or poorly on your job

No Way Of Knowing	Almost To No Way Knowing	To a Some Extent	Large Extent	Great Extent	Entirely Extent

Performance Appraisal Policy

When you /your organization develop the Performance Appraisal (PA) policy be sure to include and/or make mention of the following points:

- ☑ PA's start with a good Job Description.
- ☑ PA's can be written or verbal… Written is best.
- ☑ PA's can be quarterly, semi-annually or annually… Should be, at least annually.

Purpose

- ☑ PA's are a two-way communication between employer and employee.
- ☑ PA's can help develop the quality of the workforce (employees).
- ☑ PA's recognize the efficient and effective performance of an employee.

- ☑ PA's point out the weaknesses of an employee.
- ☑ PA's foster teamwork in an organization.
- ☑ PA's can give the employee a high degree of job satisfaction.
- ☑ PA's can fulfil the career potential of employees.
- ☑ PA's can improve productivity and professionalism.
- ☑ PA's demonstrate concern and caring for an individual.
- ☑ PA's can match an individual's talents with the right job.
- ☑ PA's can develop a continuity of information in-spite of turnovers.
- ☑ PA's develop a link for providing feedback.
- ☑ PA's can identify training needs.

Performance Appraisals – A summary

The paragraphs above have covered the Job Description, Competency Profile and Training Needs Analysis…some key ingredients of a Performance Appraisal. But for the Performance Appraisal to be an effective **management tool** the Manager/Director must also introduce, and implement, a system of undertaking Performance Appraisals. The next few paragraphs will provide some direction on how to develop the PA system.

What does a Performance Appraisal cover?

- Background and Educational Qualifications (included in job description).
- Key job duties that are mutually understood (included in the job description).
- Rating of Performance (measured against expectations in the competency profile).
- Career Potentials and Plans (an outcome of the employee review).
- Confidential Evaluation Reports (maintained in the personnel file).
-

Different Approaches to Performance Appraisals:

Certainly the component that interests, and in some cases concerns everybody the most, is the actual staff or Personnel Evaluation. This is the document that informs the employee how s/he has performed his/her duties in the eyes of the Manager/Director (supervisor). Emotions range from uncertainty to fear and apprehension to anger. It shouldn't be that way.

If there has been good *two-way* communication between the 'boss' and the employee, during the period under review (review period could be annually or quarterly) then there shouldn't be too many surprises. If there are surprises then this is an additional aspect for both the employee and employer to work on...Before the next evaluation period. Improved Performance Appraisals will go a long way in strengthening the team and should be considered as a part of the team building exercises.

One suggestion on ways to reduce the *surprise factor* is to have the evaluation more frequently, perhaps quarterly, and increase the communication between employee/employer, especially in the areas where there is disagreement or differences of opinion.

You can classify the appraisals as *official* and *informal,* both are good and both approaches can be used during the same evaluation period. The organization structure and Performance Appraisal Policy determines which approach (es) are to be taken.

Informal

- ☑ Continues Throughout The Year.
- ☑ Based On The Observation Of The Supervisor.
- ☑ Day-To-Day (Or Project To Project) Evaluation.
- ☑ Written Summary of Any Personnel Discussions.

Official

- ☑ Once a Year.
- ☑ Based On Total Performance Throughout The Year.
- ☑ Written Comments on Official Evaluation Form.

Author's favourite way to do Staff Performance

Appraisals

1. Start with a good Job Description, which includes a note under *duties* that says, "The employee will undertake any other duty as requested by the Director."
2. Personnel Evaluations are a combination of quarterly and annual reviews. Delegate the quarterly evaluations to department heads/senior supervisory personnel, using a simplified format called: Smile... S=Skills; M =Motivation; I=Inter-Personal Skills; L=Language; E=Emotional Stability. Use simple/short responses. Example: Skills – Good or Fair...Motivation – Adequate or Poor, etc.
3. Annual evaluations are intense, cover weaknesses, suggested areas for improvement, provides motivation to do better, identify training needs, and provides an opportunity for documented praise when an employee has done well.

Sample Draft Evaluation Form

All Personnel (staff) Evaluations should be confidential and the forms should be kept in Confidential Personnel Files. The evaluations go with the employee, in case of transfer to another office/department, and are part of a permanent history record of the employee. The evaluation forms should not leave the Manager's/Director's office where the evaluation is given and the evaluation should always be signed by both the employee and the employer. If there is a Grievance Committee in the organization the evaluation can be discussed, in part, with this committee if the grievance arises from the evaluation results. Local laws should be checked and legal regulations incorporated in the evaluation process/forms to ensure they comply with local laws and/or headquarters (parent organization) regulations.

The evaluation measures the performance gains or lack of performance of the employee. The outcome (performance) shows strengths and weaknesses of the employee. Everybody thinks they are doing great; the evaluation should either prove or disprove this feeling. Often the evaluation is subjective (he is a nice guy), when it should be objective (s/he has completed all of the assigned tasks including, etc.). **The evaluation should record progress by the employee, and the results of the evaluation used to motivate the employee to do better.**

The hardest part for the evaluator is separating his/her personal feelings form the employee (I really like this person and s/he is my friend) and make an unbiased evaluation of the person's achievements/performance. On the other hand, rarely should an employee's performance be rated excellent.

The Evaluation Form should include

1. Name: Date of Hire: Years in Current Position: 2. Performance by Task (in order of priority): Example: Writing of reports: Excellent... Very good... Good... Fair... Poor. 3. Overall performance (can be written): Example: Mr. Q reports to the office at the scheduled hour and doesn't waste time. He helps others when asked by his colleagues etc. 4. Suggested Areas for Improvement: Example: Ms. Y should improve her computer skills to include power point, then a salary increase will be considered. 5. Salary Increase: I think every employee should receive a minimum 3- 5 % salary increase just because s/he has served the organization for 12 months. You reward the productive employees with higher increases. 6. Next Review Period: Can be an interim (quarterly), if there are doubts about employee/performance/ability to do the job.

7. Employment Statement: An opportunity for the employee to make a signed, written statement about performance, the evaluation, and any other job-related comment that s/he wants to make.

2.2.12. Goal Setting and Planning

Remember before you can set good goals you must provide a 'vision' of what you want to achieve.

The setting of project goals and planning is as important for establishing a spirit of cooperation and positive working environment as it is for identifying and communicating the organization's activities and vision.

There are a lot of ways to prepare your plans...From prepared planning formats designed by the organization itself to the universally accepted log frame. The Manager/ Programme Director should select or design the most suitable planning format for his/her programme. Goal setting is probably better when undertaken as a team effort...as they say "two heads are better than one."

Advantage of Setting Goals as a Team

- Each team member has an opportunity to contribute, learn, and grow.
- Everyone will have a clear sense of what is expected/results to be achieved.
- The goals will have team ownership and support for the goals; and
- Implementation will be smoother with the team members supporting each other to achieve these goals.

What is needed to Set Goals and Prepare Plans?

☑ A practical idea...based on needs, supported by research and with clear, measurable objectives.

☑ Availability of resources (money, people, equipment) to carry out the activities to achieve your goals.

- ☑ Flexibility in your planning to allow for the unexpected and other changes (political/donors) that may occur.

Criteria for Setting Realistic Goals

Your goals should meet the following criteria:

- ☑ Clear and Specific
- ☑ Attainable
- ☑ Measurable
- ☑ Time Structured
- ☑ Flexible

Questions to Ask Yourself/Team When Setting Goals

- ☑ How feasible is your plan?
- ☑ Are the objectives realistic?
- ☑ What obstacles/barriers do you foresee?
- ☑ How will you measure your plans?
- ☑ How often will you monitor/evaluate your plans?
- ☑ What resources will you require/use?

2.2.13. Negotiation

Negotiation should be a management style, not a confrontational event. Also, negotiating is built on steps – start by being humble.

Overview

Most things in life are negotiable...or so the saying goes! The following paragraphs will provide you with the highlights of what it takes to be a good negotiator and a *peek* into the art of negotiation. The seven basic aspects of negotiating are commonly considered to be:

The Art of Negotiation
Establish Trust
Obtain Information
Meet Needs
Use your Opponent's Ideas

Establish A Continuing Relationship
Take Moderate Risks
Ask For And Get Your Opponent's Help

Steps for Becoming a Good Negotiator:

- Be well prepared and know what you plan to say. Have a good understanding on how you will ask intelligent questions to gain information from your opponent. This will help you discover the real limits of your opponent's position and what s/he is trying to obtain from your side.
- Perhaps you can role-play with your staff before going into negotiations. This will provide you with some reality to the pending negotiation and strengthen your ability to *seek out* the who, what, why, how and when of a situation in a better way.
- Be prepared to negotiate...and constantly seeking ways to resolve *conflict*. You should be fully conversant with the *why* and *how* disagreements are developed and how to resolve the situations.

Points to Remember When Negotiating:

- To recognize when you are in a negotiation process... and that everything negotiated is negotiable.
- Negotiation is a give and take... All parties must be satisfied before you leave the negotiating table.
- To recognize that the opponent's needs should never be completely satisfied if your needs are not completely satisfied.
- Know how to be persuasive...when to push...and when to back off. Recognize what points do not appear to be negotiable.
- Some cultures do not place emphasis on signed, written contracts and agreements at the conclusion of a negotiation as do western cultures—Where they tend to become the law as a legal document. In some cultures,

"A signed contract is a good place to start negotiations."

Part Two

Organization, Programme and Project Design and Set-up

1 Getting Started

Overview

For the purpose of this Handbook the **organization** is defined as the **entity or the NGO.** The **programme** is defined as the undertaking and implementation of **several different projects** and a **project** is the individual **development activity** or intervention.

The organization will require a base of operation in which to operate its programmes. The organization will also be required to write proposals to get funding for projects and equip an office and train the staff. The organization will require a Manager/Director to head the office and also manage the programme and projects.

That person, who is responsible for the management of the projects is the **'undressed Manager,'** and thus this handbook is designed keeping him/her in mind.

The designing and setting up of an organization and subsequent programme, requires money and guidelines, usually provided by the main or headquarters office. Designing projects is something quite different and has many requirements, here are just a few.

Designing a Project

- ☑ The Project Needs must be identified. These needs are often based on donor or governments perception...and verified by research or needs assessments.
- ☑ The needs must fall under the mandate of the donor or parent organization.
- ☑ The project requires vision of the Manager/Director.

- ☑ The project must identify available resources (funding/human/physical) for Project Implementation.
- ☑ The community, politicians, religious leaders, government officials, and other partners must be involved in these projects.
- ☑ The project must demonstrate aspects of sustainability.

All projects require funding...and to get funding one must often prepare a Project Proposal. Proposals can be unsolicited, and presented to potential donors for funding, or prepared in response to an advertised request for proposals (RFP). Unsolicited proposals can, at times, be preceded by a *concept paper,* which briefly outlines the proposed project. The RFPs are based on a ToR, and usually issued by the donor or host government.

Regardless, if the proposals are unsolicited or in response to an RFP, the following basic structure applies:

1.1. Proposal Writing

Key components of a proposal

- Background
- Statement of Problem
- Methodology
- Implementation Steps
- Work Plan or Time Line
- Staffing or Personnel
- Previous Relevant Experience
- Log Frame
- Financial Proposal

1.2 Components of a Technical Proposal

Background...This is usually the first section in a technical proposal; this section either covers the previous or ongoing project activities or states how the new project came into being and describes briefly the reasons for initiating the new activity; this section also identifies the geographical location of where the activities are being implemented, explains how the project is/was being implemented and by whom (government/ partners) and why the project should be started or continued; this section should include data or achievements and expected future results.

Key points to cover in Background Statement
• Demonstrate your knowledge of the country conditions and needs.
• Provide relevant data/statistics on the Project Needs.
• Indicate your organization's experience/expertise to implement the project activities.
• Acknowledge sources of background statements/data (UN reports, government sources).
• Include graphics/charts to show severity of problems and escalating problems (example: increasing HIV prevalence).
• Include demographic trends to support planned project areas.
• Highlight unusual situations (40% population below poverty line) for effect and project justification.

Problem Statement...This usually follows the *background* section and can build on many of the points (needs, purpose of the project) identified in the background section; the *Problem Statement* generally, describes in detail the existing or felt needs of the target group or intended beneficiaries of the project; and presents the *problem* to be solved with the implementation of the activity. Problem statements should contain good reliable data and statistics in support of the project; a Problem Statement should clearly state what is needed...and/or what is the actual problem; examples of the *Problem* in a Problem Statement could include: Malnutrition, child abuse, high HIV prevalence rates, etc. and should clearly illustrate what the problem is ...including the causes of the problem, impact the problem may have/is having on the country, the youth, its economy, etc.

Key Points to cover in the Problem Statement
• Severity of the situation in country (HIV prevalence/ high MMR).

• Lack of equipment, materials, human resources in country.
• Increasing negative impact on economic development.
• Inability of government resources to fully tackle the problem.
• Ongoing efforts do not reach all the population.

Methodology...This is considered by many donors as the most important section of the proposal (after the proposed personnel/consultants). In this section the writer must describe very clearly how you are going to approach the problem, what you are going to do (activities to be implemented) and how you will solve the problem; what ways, what methods, systems and techniques...that you are going to use in solving the problem; how will you build on the existing programmes or utilize local structures to solve the problem; how you will use other partners and government resources; how you will make the project sustainable; what strategies will be used; how you plan to monitor and evaluate the activities.

Key Points to cover in the Methodology
• How will you implement the project (CBD approach or?).
• Where will the project be implemented (urban, high risk group)?
• Who will be involved, How they will be involved in the implementation (NGOs)?
• How long will the implementation take...By years/phases?
• Show how your selected implementation method compliments the ongoing efforts/programmes of government/others.

Implementation Steps...Sometimes this section is also called the *general approach* or *plan of action*; it is here that you describe how you will undertake the project and where you will start (first *step* is perhaps by doing a study or review of the ongoing programme activities); then the next *step* is what follows after the study/review is completed and so on, until you have completed all the *steps* necessary to implement the project and reach the goals/objectives. This section shows how the project activities (steps) flow one after another... How they integrate into other ongoing similar projects; how these steps lead towards reaching the project objectives, including sustainability; what results have been achieved; and an indication of how and when monitoring is to be undertaken; and when the evaluations are scheduled.

Key Points to cover in the Implementation Steps
• Implementation should be a detailed work plan of activities.
• Place activities in step-by-step order... Hire and train staff, under take quantitative/qualitative research, assessment of ongoing activities, development of implementation systems, etc.
• Provide a time frame/manning schedule of people/activities.
• Show links with other/ongoing programmes.
• Identify partners... Show ways of collaboration.
• Outline reporting schedule... Monthly, quarterly, annual.

Needs Assessment... Many proposal writers will include, as a part of the implementation steps, a Needs Assessment. It usually requires research or some type of surveys for accomplishment.

Key Points to cover in the Needs Assessment
• Show how the new project will meet the *needs* by linking to the MDGs or Global Initiatives if the project is implemented.
• Show how your project will integrate the activities into the national programme to accomplish the government's needs better.
• Make a summary review of financial resource allocations to implement the project...'X' amount for equipment/medicines to fulfil the needs.
• Indicate how your organization and resources – human and financial will be used to overcome the needs.

Work Plan and Time Line... Work plans can also be known as **a manning schedule,** this section is usually presented as a chart/table, accompanied by a short narrative description; this section should cover the planned activities in the sequence and time frame to be completed; the work plan will include the project goals and objectives, inputs and outcomes; the manning chart will identify the local and external consultants being hired for project implementation; indicate where and how this work plan compliments/supplements the government's national action plan and how these plans will lead towards sustainability; link the responsible person (manning chart) to the activity; link implementation of the activity to a specific time period (A sample work plan can be found in the Annex of this handbook).

Project Personnel... Donors/funding agencies usually pay most attention to this section and thoroughly review the quality and relevant experience of the staff/consultants assigned to the implementation of the project; therefore it's a good idea to weave the expertise of the staff into the implementation steps of the proposal and also include a brief summary of each professional's background and relevant experience somewhere in the body of the proposal; the Personnel section should be prepared showing the titles, roles and a brief professional description. Usually complete CVs are included in the annex, which is also a good place to include the organization's expertise and capabilities.

Key Points to cover in Project Personnel
• Show clearly where your staff has the required previous experience/expertise...Give details of achievements/ projects.
• Indicate availability, cultural sensitivity, language skills, knowledge of latest technology and capacity building skills.

Previous Relevant Experience... When writing the proposal assume that the readers know nothing about your organization... So include every detail, especially past experience in the country/region/globally. Highlight your achievements, show similarities between what is the need in this project and what you have accomplished in previous projects. Use photos to compliment your description... and don't forget to include what impact/results you have achieved on the target group. At the end of this section it's also nice to show lessons learned...and assure the reader that you won't be reinventing the wheel again or be wasting time/money during implementation.

Key Points to cover in Previous Relevant Experience
• Show your technical staff's past experiences too.
• Highlight senior staff's knowledge of area/technical subject.
• Show past involvement in similar projects...Use project photos, press articles, credits from other donors for doing a good job.

Log Frame... The Log Frame is usually a part of any technical proposal and provides a visual planning overview of the complete project (goals, outcomes, inputs, indicators etc); the log frame helps the writer think through the execution, expectations and obstacles of the project while writing the other sections of the proposal; the log frame is expected to show *logically* the outcomes when activities/inputs are provided; the log frame also identifies the project objectives, activities to be implemented, expected results, possible barriers, indicators and ways/how to verify the results (a sample log frame can be found in the Annex of this handbook).

Financial Proposal... Often bound and submitted separately from the technical proposal; many times donors will specify how they want the financial proposal prepared and in what format; also be prepared to produce and include verification of experts salaries, and audited overheads; usually the financial proposal is broken down into direct and indirect project costs (including programme and administrative costs); the financial proposal will include equipment purchases, depreciation schedules and costs for undertaking audits; at times additional documentation is required like tax records, salary history of staff, audit reports, banking information and proof of financial solvency; total costs are often itemized separately by operations, personnel, equipment and administrative costs.

Project Designs should be

- Clearly written
- Easy to read
- Complete in details
- Relevant
- Unique

Key points to cover in the Finance Section
☑ Detail costs by activity (staff/materials/equipment) to show where funds are being spent (and not only on overheads/salaries). Also, in case you have to cut the budget to be competitive it's easier to know where the *fat* (excess) is.
☑ Indicate any cost recovery aspects and/or contributions in kind.
☑ Indicate what financial needs you will have... Duty free, office space to be provided by counterpart and transport.
☑ Indicate the project will be audited...and give frequency

Often projects are bid in competition with other organizations, thus your financial proposal should reflective competitive costs for undertaking the project. Leave some rooms for reducing the total cost of your services... Donors seldom accept the first price offered by the bidding organization.

1.3 Elements of a Project Design

The heart of your programme is your project activities. In the designing of your new projects, you and your team will have to consider several different elements that will have to be addressed, perhaps even researched, before you prepare your project proposal.

1.3.1 The Main Elements to Consider:

a. **Beneficiaries (Target Audience)**...Who are they (if kids, what age group); where do they live (rural or urban); special cases (orphans, HIV +).

b. **Geographical Location**...will the projects be country wide or only select areas; are the projects reaching the poorest of the poor or the greatest population density; will there be a pilot study to introduce a new concept/project approach.

c. **Quality Assurance Standards**... Quality assurance can apply to equipment and/or international standards, for, say, child protection; quality assurance measures can be identified in international agreements (CRC, for example) or as international specifications, which is the case in AIDS prevention to ensure only high quality contraceptives are procured.

d. **Training Needs**... Training is ongoing throughout the life of your project; training starts with day one of your programme operations; training is best if conducted in the local language and by persons familiar with not only the technical subject but also the country conditions and the goals of the programme; external training is often required and budgeted for on an annual basis; training is for everyone...From the driver up to the most senior officer.

e. **Finance**... 'Money talks or nobody walks'... an old adage that applies to all programmes and organizations; donors are necessary and need to be identified before the organization is set up or programmes begin...or shortly, thereafter, depending on the situation at the time; everyone should be involved in donor relations and funding raising activities; your visibility (PR) materials should be appealing to donors with clear and concise programme and project details; continued follow up and reporting to donors is essential and a major part of the programme Manager's ongoing responsibilities. Always keep the donor informed.

f. **Research/Surveys**... Most household and consumer data is unreliable, and economic data can be manipulated to create the desired image... Therefore, each programme should begin with some initial surveys and/or studies; studies should be prepared by local professionals...Statisticians (for sampling size) and questionnaire design and pre-testing by social scientists...analysis of findings by both, and perhaps an economist too; the decision to collect quantitative or qualitative data...or both...should be made depending on the project needs/design.

g. **Compliance**...Pertains to Quality Assurance (see above) and also to National Norms and International Conventions; International Standards can be found in the CRC and CEDAW conventions, in the PRSP, UNAIDS country reports, UNDP country profiles, the MDGs, and numerous others; all Programme Managers should familiarize themselves with these conventions and standards and ensure compliance in their technical proposals.

h. **Sustainability**... Addressing issues of Project Sustainability is an element that must be included in all project designs; cost recovery, more efficient operations, and better resource utilization can all lead to a more sustainable project.

Project Design and Management Cycle

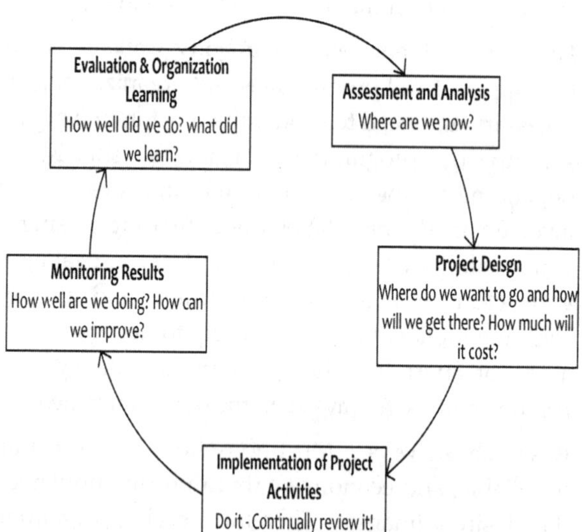

1.4 Programme and Project Structure

The structure of the overall programme will be influenced a lot by your headquarters or main office policies, advisory boards and the philosophy of that organization.

But the project structure will be determined by activities that:

1. are a part of the host government's National Programme.
2. addresses the MDGs.
3. are within the implementation capacities of the newly formed organization.
4. have elements of sustainability.

Project activity selection can also be based on:

- previous, successful project implementation by and/or affiliate offices.
- successful activities of other NGOs working in country.
- specific requests from the host government and/or donors.
- needs outlined by the communities where the organization is operating.

1.5 Designing the New Programme and Projects

When designing your new programme/projects you want to look internally, at what the government and other organizations are doing, as well as externally, to gain an understanding of the international community's involvement in the country's development activities.

To begin with, you may wish to ask yourself these questions

- ☑ What projects are already being implemented/ funded?
- ☑ Where is the niche for your organization to work?
- ☑ What do you bring special to the development projects?
- ☑ Can you find funding sources?
- ☑ What level of sustainability can the project achieve?

Can your new organization operate/function under the various policies/conventions currently existing?

Part of the project design phase will include integrating your project activities into ongoing national programmes.

Please see Chapter 3, Part 2, Section 3.6 Partners and Donors, where we discuss working with partners and integrating your proposed projects into the local Government's National Plan. Also refer to the Project Design and Management Cycle Chart to review the design flow.

It may be considered unwise to undertake any project that is not part of the Government's National Programme. It is also the smart programme/project Manager who knows what other development projects are being supported by donors/NGOs and are currently being implemented.

1.6 Building on Existing Strengths for a Stronger Programme

When planning and developing your programme strategy and projects, try to incorporate ongoing approaches and methodologies...that have worked. The trick, of course, is to find what has worked. A good Manager will try to learn from the experiences of others, be aware of the potential barriers/obstacles and don't make the same mistakes.

Some Programme Building Tips

a. **Focus your work areas**... Identify where you can make a difference, undertake activities that fit into your programme mission statement and where you have the funding and expertise to implement the activities.

b. **Select projects that donors are likely to fund**... Know your potential donors well...meet them informally and/or formally... Don't discuss specific business details in the first meeting... Donor solicitation is like dating... Get to know each other before you ask for a good night kiss...and don't waste their time...or yours...by discussing projects that they can't or won't fund...or that you can't implement.

c. **Partnerships**... The right partner will strengthen your proposal and facilitate implementation of the project activities;

some partner selection is based on political consideration, but others (majority) should be selected on what they can contribute to Project Implementation; clearly identify who is the lead partner, assign responsibilities to each partner before discussing with potential donors; partners should be complimentary and supplementary to your overall development approach.

d. **Expertise within the organization**... In-house expertise is easier to manage and control...as well as more cost effective; partners can train your existing staff to build up your in-house capabilities; consider what expertise you will need when hiring new staff; conduct in-house training to strengthen the expertise amongst all staff.

e. **Needs of beneficiaries**... Problem Identification is step one in results based management...so you need to know your beneficiaries; you must know their needs as well as their capabilities to assist in Project Implementation; assess the cost of your needs to determine what donor inputs are essential; knowledge of what technical inputs you will need is critical, and can be a guide in your partner selection.

f. **Review Evaluations**... Before embarking on any new project activity, review the evaluation comments and recommendations of what was previously attempted; knowledge is power; assess the indicators previously used for monitoring performance and impact; learn the lessons from other's experiences.

g. **Personnel Management**... Taking care of your human resource investment, and keeping the same staff (team) members is key to building programme and project strengths and capabilities; building human resources is an expensive investment and efforts to keep and motivate existing staff is money well spent; donors are more convinced to support your efforts if they see the same in-house expertise being used repeatedly; in today's development environment a Manger must think about 'AIDS in the workplace' training, to protect your staff and your investment in them.

2
Organizational Design

Overview

Now that you have the funding to implement the project it's time to set up the infrastructure–human, administrative and physical - necessary to properly carry out the program and project activities. The following guidelines and suggestions...albeit at times, perhaps, over simplified...should get you started.

In setting up an organisation, everything is important... But always keep in mind that every action and/or decision you take is:

- ☑ within the laws of the country.
- ☑ in line with the mandate of the parent organization and donor.
- ☑ within the budget and financial limitations of the project proposal; and
- ☑ focused on achieving the goals and objectives of the headquarters office and as identified in the technical proposal...and for which you have been allocated the funds.

2.1 Defining the Organization's Purpose

Each new organization should set for itself the following:
Vision Statement; and **Mission Statement**

Thinking about and preparing these two statements will not only help you focus on why you are here but what you hope to achieve.

Vision Statement: The best way to define a vision statement is...'What do you SEE (or dream) happening in the future'...within the organization...with the resources available...and what benefits do you see for the people/communities you are working with. Simply ask these questions to yourself and you will come up with a pretty good vision statement.

Examples:

For a Safe Drinking Water Project:

"*Happier and healthier children because they don't have worms!*"

For a Child Nutrition Project:

"*Mothers will be comforted knowing their children are growing up strong.*"

The organization must have a vision, but so must the Manager/Director. It is his/her vision that will provide direction and move the programme forward.

Mission Statement: Mission Statements generally indicate/define what the organization hopes to **accomplish** and **achieve**... It defines your purpose in being here, and why you are starting an organization. Mission Statements can also be used as organization mottos, and unlike Vision Statements, are generally printed on public relation materials and letter head paper.

Part of your organization's Mission Statement can include the purpose behind establishing the programme, a mention of the activities and/or the community will benefit.

Examples:

For a Community based Development Programme:

"*Improving the quality of life together!*"

For a Health Programme:

"*Reducing Health Risks for All!*"

2.2 Forming an Organization

Quite simply...You wish to establish an organization (legal entity) that will have a presence in country (a specific location) which will undertake several different activities (projects)...and these collective projects will be known as the *programme*.

The registration of this new organization can be structured as an NGO, Foundation, Non-Profit Organization, etc. (see box below) and may even have field offices, located outside the capital city.

The organization will have different functions - administrative and logistical support, fund raising, public relations, advocacy, and financial support. The organization may also provide technical backstopping in support of the several different development projects.

The projects will be implemented as per the Project Proposal, which are funded by donors. Combined projects make up the *programme*.

Illustrative Example

Legal Entity (NGO, foundation)	is the	Organization.
Water, Health and ECD	are the	Projects.
Digging tube wells, developing ECD materials	are the	Project Development Activities.
The ECD, water and health projects	is the	Programme.
Finance, procurement, administration	are the	Organization. Support Activities.

2.3 Structuring an Organization

The type of organization to be established will depend on the current rules and regulations governing the creation of an organization in the host country and the mandate of the local organization's advisory board.

Some donors do not want an operation (a parallel programme) set-up outside the local government structure. Also governments and donors alike do not want to see vertical programmes established. Usually a non-profit NGO is the most common way to begin.

Other options to consider include:

1. **GONGO**.... The host government or a government official(s) who is involved with the formation and operation of a locally established NGO.
2. **Not-for-profit Organisation**... A legal entity that could be established along the lines of an NGO or Foundation that is permitted to generate revenues/income, but not make a profit.
3. **Limited Liability Corporation**.... A legal entity that charges fees for services *non-profit* in structure, and with limited liabilities for its actions.
4. **Commercial Organisation**...that is *profit*-oriented in nature and designed along the lines of a commercial organization, but is humanitarian (social) in its project activities.

2.4 Visibility Plans

Visibility in the context of this handbook is considered promotion (public relations) of the programme and/or your project activities. This would include the advertising and promotion of your logo design, mottos, mission statements, and creating brand (name) recognition.

Visibility is essential for awareness and conveying information to the general public of what the organization is doing and can do...and for educating the donor on the organization's experience, expertise, skills and project development focus.

Each organization/programme should attempt to be visible in as many ways as possible, by using the ways mentioned below…or creating new ones.

Ways to Increase Visibility

Visibility could be achieved through:

- presentations…at workshops or seminars.
- advocacy at public forums.
- promotional advertisements in newspapers/ magazines.
- TV and radio sponsorship.
- sign boards at project sites.
- billboards and hoardings; and
- the more traditional printed publications: Brochures and Leaflets.

Producing materials for information dissemination and donor education is an expensive undertaking, and if you are not careful can produce a negative image.

Developing a Visibility Plan

The visibility plan for the organization, the programme and the projects should contain different messages, be designed differently and promoted in varying ways. The main reasons being, information about the programme will be more general in nature, provide the philosophy (vision and mission statements) of the organization; and reflect the skills/expertise and management capabilities of the organization as a whole.

In the Project Visibility Plan the *promotional highlights* will be more on the achievements, systems, products, impact, benefits and methodology of the project. A Project Visibility Plan will show what it took to implement the project…and the accomplishments.

	Things to Look for in Developing All Visibility Materials
a)	What is the most effective way to get your message across to the intended audience? How best to disseminate the information?
b)	What is the most cost effective method to use?
c)	What is the most appropriate language to use? Is more than one language necessary?
d)	What format or design layout should be used?
e)	Can these be printed/prepared locally...In country...outside the country? Compare cost and quality of materials. How will you distribute the printed materials?
f)	Is the text, design, colour and content culturally sensitive? What kind of image is being presented? Does the material create or reinforce 'brand' recognition?
g)	Is the material factual, relevant, useful and easy to read?
h)	What is unique about the organization and/or project achievements? Is this clearly brought out in the promotional materials?
i)	Is this a 'one-off' use or something that can be used again?

3 Setting-up an Office

3.1 Locating an office... Things to consider when selecting a new office

- ☑ Will the client/donor provide office space?
- ☑ How far is the office from the main counterpart's office?
- ☑ How does the office fit into the organization's image?
- ☑ Should you use an estate agent to find an office or place an advertisement in the paper yourself?
- ☑ What is 'normally' provided by the landlord?
- ☑ Is there ample room for secure parking of office vehicles?
- ☑ Should a lawyer review the lease before signing?
- ☑ Are rents going to increase/decrease over the life of the project?
- ☑ Is the office presentable to your visitors?
- ☑ Is there room for additional staff or expansion?
- ☑ Is there privacy and comfortable work spaces?
- ☑ Is there a *flow* in the office for good communications?
- ☑ Is electricity supply adequate for the planned equipment?
- ☑ Will telephone lines handle internet connections?
- ☑ Is there sufficient money in the budget to cover rent/utilities?
- ☑ Can you obtain a beneficial discount by taking a long term lease?

3.2 Setting up the Organization's Operations.

- ☑ Open a bank account... Check with donors/auditors for signatory powers. Are monthly bank statements provided? Do you have online banking facility?

- ☑ Procure office furniture... Obtain at least three quotations. Do you import or buy locally? Will the landlord provide some furniture?
- ☑ Procure vehicles... Check for duty free permission/requirements. Determine the need of four wheel drive vehicles. Check availability of spare parts/qualified mechanics.
- ☑ Meet counterparts/partners... Follow protocols (appointments/introductions). Dress properly, and remember cultural norms.
- ☑ Assign office space...including car parking areas. Consider office flow, privacy and any special arrangements (security of finance person if cash is kept in the office, location of conference room for noise factor).
- ☑ Set up computer network and obtain a server. Set-up a common printer to reduce costs.
- ☑ Review local rules/regulations/laws... including tax and labour laws. Put up a notice board to publicly display certificates/legal registration.
- ☑ Establish office timings/holiday lists and office hours.
- ☑ Establish office/work policies and procedures...an ongoing task.

3.3. Contracts and Contract Negotiations

During the setting up of an office, and implementing subsequent project activities, the Manager will be involved in the preparation and signing of various legal contracts.

Some of these documents, like a Memorandum of Understanding (MoU) or employee agreement, will not have direct financial implications...others, like procurement contracts will. Some things to remember when preparing, and before signing a legal document, are:

- ☑ Have a lawyer review the document before signing?
- ☑ Obtain necessary approvals from parent organization/ donor.

- ☑ Make sure the document complies to local laws, including import and duty free conditions.
- ☑ Be sure there is money budgeted to cover any costs described in the document, and a schedule of payments.
- ☑ If procuring equipment please ensure installation terms and product guarantees are included in the agreement.
- ☑ Ensure the organization is protected from any legal action, including environmental damage or personal injury.
- ☑ With employee agreements, ensure the contract is in compliance to local labour and tax laws.

3.4. Equipment Procurement

Equipment Procurement is becoming more difficult, in part because this is an area of great concern for most donors. Usually large sums of money are involved in procuring the new equipment, and transparency in procuring the equipment has become very important to all parties.

Likewise, an equal sum of money is also required for maintenance and running costs. And this has become a concern for both the donor and the recipient of the equipment.

Please be sure to check the procurement requirements in the contract before you decide to do anything. These procurement conditions should cover everything from minimum number of quotations to be obtained to who must give the final approval for the purchase. Country of origin, duty exempt facilities, payment/money transfer procedures and specifications are common issues.

More and more there is a question of *ownership* of the equipment. Who is responsible for maintaining the equipment, who can use the equipment (especially true for vehicles) during the life of the project and who gets the equipment when the project comes to an end?

Vehicles are usually the single biggest purchase, and questions like country of origin (many donors require that you buy from the country which is providing the fund)…To who pays the duty, if not duty exempt. Questions can even be raised about what type of license plate should be put on the vehicle (some countries have special NGO or technical assistance license plates). All these issues can cause the Manager/Director headaches if procedures are not followed correctly. Someone once said, "Wives and vehicles are a Manager's biggest headache."

Some Procurement Tips

- ☑ Read the project contract…. If in doubt contact the donor.
- ☑ Understand the importation laws of the country.
- ☑ Get all the necessary paper work in order before ordering.
- ☑ Ensure that translations into local languages are official.
- ☑ Use a procurement agency if needed.
- ☑ Be familiar with other brands of equipment used in country.
- ☑ Check on international specifications for the equipment.
- ☑ Ensure electrical and interface connections are compatible.
- ☑ Enquire if repair technicians are located in the project area.
- ☑ Ascertain the spare parts availability BEFORE purchasing.
- ☑ Have a lawyer review Procurement Agreements.
- ☑ Have an agreement on ownership/disposal.
- ☑ Have a policy in place on equipment use.

3.5. Filling Human Resource Needs

Human Resource Development (capacity building) is an ongoing activity for the **'undressed Manager.'** Building a strong and solid team is an investment, which will enhance the image of the organization, ensure better project implementation and increase the opportunities for project sustainability.

3.5.1. Steps in Building a Team are as Follows

- Develop a good criteria (qualifications) for each office/project position, put them in writing for everyone to see.
- Advertise the positions widely–in local and national newspapers, electronic media and on website.

- Set-up good interviewing techniques – make a short list of candidates and form a solid selection committee.
- Establish an Interview questionnaire and conduct tests, if appropriate.
- Select, screen and hire the right people from the beginning.
- Provide each new employee a detailed Job Description.
- Undertake Performance Appraisals (evaluations) on a regular basis.
- Hold regular team meetings for better communication.
- Provide on-the-job or external training for skills development.
- Find ways to motivate the team, other than monetary basis.
- The Manager must provide the **<u>Leadership</u>** and direction for any team.

3.6. Office Policies and Procedures

Policies are the approved operating guidelines, which should be set by the Manager and followed by all staff/team members. Policies are:

- Generally developed based on proven strategies, should conform to the overall organizational policies and any specific donor requirements.
- Must be approved by the Manager/Director, or perhaps by the parent organization, donor or host government counterpart
- Need to be formulated from day one (hiring policy/new staff, office hours, etc.) and established in a transparent manner.
- Can be formulated in several different ways - based on management style, local conditions and existing circumstances.
- Need to be enforced…and responsible person(s) in-charge of enforcement identified (example: Office Administrator enforces the policy on getting to work at the scheduled time).

- Must be circulated/posted to all staff members ...and/or shared with the partner/donor as appropriate.
- Policies can cover both internal and external operations.
- Need to be flexible and revised/changed/dropped as the situation dictates.

Procedures relate more to Operational Systems. Once a procedure is set-up and working it can become a policy.

- What procedure (what steps) is set-up and followed for the flow of fax messages received in the office, what are the procedures to be followed when advertising for new staff...What are the procedures (process) for complaining about the boss's mistreatment of a staff member.
- Like policies, procedures need to be established early on in the setting up of a new office/programme.
- Procedures should be approved by the Manager/Director.
- Procedures are most often applied to internal organizational operations.
- Procedures should be written down, circulated and displayed.

3.6.1 Some Important Office Policies and Procedures

Office Policies

- Working days/hours, lunch break, visitors hours, and holiday lists, dress codes.
- Leave Policy – number of days of sick leave, annual holidays, personal leave.
- Policy on overtime, compensatory time off.
- Personal and official use of vehicles, office equipment (photo copy, computer, internet), use of long distance phone/fax lines.
- Training- internal and external, and capacity building, including time for attending advanced degree courses.
- Team building, including social activities.

- Hiring, firing and promotion policies.
- Scheduling and use of conference room.
- Personnel Evaluations and Performance Appraisals.
- Signing of documents/contracts and agreements.
- Procurement policies.
- Correspondence style/format and use of letter head paper.
- Inner-office communication/memos.

Office Procedures

- Setting up appointments to meet the Project Manager or for contacting donors or partners.
- Requesting the procurement of office supplies.
- Procedures for setting up an office bank account/ payments.
- Procedures for requesting leave, salary advances, per diem claims.
- Procedures for submitting personal grievances.

3.7 Organization and Method (O&M)

- **O&M investigates the efficiency in an organization. O&M looks at:**
- Organization Structure
- Controls
- Information Systems
- Operational Methods
- **O&M is used to:**
- Eliminate Unnecessary Work
- Simplify the Work
- Reduce Costs
- Increase Efficiency and Productivity
- **O&M can be applied for:**
- Setting up Filing and Record Keeping Systems.
- Designing the Office Layout/Plan.

- Designing various Forms (donor reporting/internal reports).
- Selection of Office Equipment.
- **How you can use O&M to improve the efficiency in your office**

O&M will help you make decisions and find solutions. Think about your office operations for a moment...Now ask yourself these questions:

☑ What is the purpose/function of the office...Is it for support, for storage, a meeting/training place???...What can be changed to better satisfy or to improve the intended use of the office?

☑ How often is the office used for non-project related purposes (community meetings, special events)? When is it used for these purposes, and is there flexibility in the timing/use?

☑ What procedures should the office follow... Why should they be like that? Are they working? Can they be changed?

O&M is basically a checklist that makes you think about and take a hard look at the office set-up and administrative functions. By reviewing the office situation from time to time, you can improve the operating efficiency and create a better and smoother functioning environment.

4

Staffing Requirements Organization and Project

Overview

Determining the staffing needs, for both the organization (administrative) and the project (primarily technical) requires a great deal of skill, on the part of the Manager/Director. Two key points to consider:

1. Understanding of the task/activity to be performed by the employee and the necessary associated skills/knowledge required by the person who will be doing the job; and
2. How to transfer this 'understanding' into a well-written Vacancy Advertisement, an interviewing process and subsequently a clear Job Description. (Please see Part 1, Chapter 2, section 11 on Performance Appraisals).

4.1 Developing a Team

For donor and business-plan purposes, the organization can be considered as serving two roles – administrative support and indirect supervision of projects. Those working for/in the organization have a more or less permanent status, while those assigned directly to project activities are in a time-barred situation, and therefore somewhat less permanent.

The difference between organization and project is made primarily to reflect the options in office arrangements and staffing patterns, as indicated below. The following suggestions are given to provide for maximum cost efficiency, and should be adapted to local conditions and the changing organizational management needs. Management is not an exact science…Thus the staffing structures offered below are, by no means, cast in cement nor is it mandatory to follow the structure exactly as described.

4.2. Advertising and Interviewing- Steps and Roles

4.2.1 Advertising

Advertising for the various programme and administrative staff positions depends a lot on advertising budget at your disposal. Also you should consider length and breadth of the area you wish to cover, population strength and density. It is often good to use selected or targeted advertising…such as trade magazines/medical journals or websites, which are dedicated to and read by people with the skills you are looking for…It may prove to be the best way to go.

Also of importance is to make sure your adverts are on the correct page of the newspaper (employment section…not lost in some other section)…And it's best, but usually more expensive, to insert your ads on the week day that most people read a newspaper. The newspaper company or an advertising agency can provide information on when and how you might get the best coverage and results from your advert.

The message content of the advertisement should be clear to the reader. Do not use acronyms that others outside your organization might not be familiar with, and give full titles, not abbreviations of titles, and include areas of work concentration, etc. List the important terms in the advert… Position title, qualifications, location of assignment, duration, benefits, salary, reporting authority, and the like, and of course, when, how and to whom they should contact in reply. A brief description of the organization and job is also appreciated.

The more information you provide, the fewer number of telephone calls you will receive asking questions and a better quality of candidates.

After advertising and the numerous CVs have been received it is wise to make a short list (narrowing the possible candidates) down a final three or six persons for each position. Only those on the 'short list' will be interviewed. Common, these days, is to narrow down to six persons (assuming a large number replied to your advert)...and then conduct telephone interviews of these six eventually selecting three candidates for personal interviews.

4.2.2 Interviewing

The purpose of the interview for you is to gather information about that person...his/her experience, communication skills, maturity, personality and for him/her to ask questions about the job and your organization. The decision to hire the person is generally based on the result of the interview...So it is a critical process.

How to Conduct an Interview – some tips!
a) **Properly structure the interview**... Providing a proper structure improves the reliability of the interview. Plus helps to focus the discussion questions to ensure that all applicants are measured by the same criteria. In addition, a structured approach reduces the chances of any questions not being asked, and also assists the interviewer to monitor the allotted interview time. b) **Obtain evidence of candidate's past behaviour**... Interview discussions should centre around evidence and fact...not opinions voiced by the candidate. Knowing how the potential employee performed and behaved in the past is the best measure of how s/he will probably perform in your organization. Understanding his/her behaviour will also alert you as to how well the new employee will work in your team. c) **Take notes**... The interviewer, or another person sitting in on the interview, should take detailed notes. The notes should include the points/evidences provided and discussed during the interview...and what was said should be written down and note the impressions, etc.

d) **Use other interview/assessment techniques**... The interview should be supported by other assessment techniques that will give you a better understanding and ability to assess the candidate's potential. These techniques could include a written test, role play or group discussion activity.

e) **More than one person should be on the interview panel**... This is done for obvious reasons... To gather different impressions of the candidate, and to remove any possible prejudices or other biases. The interview panel should meet and discuss each candidate immediately after the interview.

Note: Many of the above points on interviewing were taken from the unicef Human Resources Guide.

4.3 Positioning of Organization/Project Staff

4.3.1 Staff Allocations

Usually organizations maintain a headquarters or country office in the country's main or capital city. To better service the projects many organizations open what we call branch or project offices. These branch/project offices are generally located directly in the project area, or at least nearby. The different offices can require different staffing needs for cost efficiency and management.

Staff positions and needs should be determined by the functions the office will perform. If this office provides mainly administrative support, then most probably you would require finance, procurement and administrative support personnel. In the branch/project office, you would probably wish to locate your technical and project management people. Rule of thumb... Let the project staff manage the projects and the administrative offices provide the necessary back-up and support.

Of course, the separation of office functions is not always black and white. There can be a lot of overlaps and other factors, including staff availability, and organizational management styles to consider. However, it is always smart to try and let the project/branch office carry out the daily project management.

They are on the spot and should be in the best position to implement the activities.

The decisions on office functions and staffing should be made by all concerned, and in a transparent manner. Regardless of how you eventually set up your office after finalisation of the office/staffing the next step is to prepare an organization chart (organigram). The organization chart and staffing structure can also be included in technical proposals, to show depth, strength and capabilities. A sample organization chart is included in the annex of this handbook.

Suggested Positions for a Country Office

- Director or Representative... Overall responsibility for all aspects of the organization, operations and programmes. Required to hire and train local field staff, develop systems and procedures for office operations and programme implementation. Maintain liaison with government counterparts, partners, donors and other stakeholders. Monitor programme activities and control financial expenditures.
- Deputy Director/Assistant Director (optional)... Similar responsibilities to the Director, with authority over specific tasks as outlined/ordered by the Director. On some occasions the Deputy can take over the programme and the Director will handle administration/finance/government liaison.
- Financial Manager... Generally number two in the office, unless there is a deputy or assistant Director. Primary tasks are planning, forecasting, maintaining and operating the financial accounts and systems, including bank statements, audits, procurement, inventory control, programme expenditures, cash flow, office petty cash, all cash receipts and disbursements and MIS.

Office Administrator/Manager... Responsible for daily office operations and communication flow, equipment (computers/photo copy) maintenance, vehicle use/log, procurement/storage of office supplies, help to establish office policies and support to the staff as needed/required. Reporting to the Director on all issues/problems.

- Office Receptionist... Assistant to (reports to) the Office Administrator, responsible for making appointments, receiving/making telephone calls and sending / recording /receiving fax messages, logistics as requested, greeting guests/officials, supervisor of office cleaning/maintenance and other tasks as described above.
- Office driver... Primarily for Director and office administration use. Responsible for main office vehicle (cleaning, servicing, repairs).
- Cleaning/cooking staff... Hired on a part-time basis, reports to the Office Administrator.

4.3.2 Suggested Positions for a Project Office

Project Staffing needs, both personnel selected/hired and the length of employment will be dictated by the actual project budget and/or project terms of reference. Project staff should be hired under the conditions and terms of the project/donor agreement only. Concise Personnel Contracts, stating the terms of employment, should be issued and clear job descriptions prepared. In some situations, it would be advised to have a lawyer review the contracts before signing.

Project staff positions will be described, and budgeted for, in the Technical Proposal. The criteria (skills, language technical capability, etc.) for the person(s) filling these positions should be well understood by all concerned and approved by the organization's Director/Representative. Titles like Project Liaison Officer or Project Coordinator should generally not be used. These titles tend to be 'fuzzy' with regards to actual responsibilities and inevitably conflict with the project Manager or other people/titles. Likewise, don't give the title of 'Manager' to some one unless s/he will actually 'manage' something...Remember there is a difference between management and supervision. Titles that define the position like...Health Project Manager or Project Engineer (water) is better.

4.3.3 Suggestions on Financial Management

Financial Management can be broken down into fiscal planning and operations. The **planning** will include the preparation of forecasts, budgeting and fund allocation, by project line items. **Operations** will cover pretty much day-to-day accounting disbursements, payments/receipts, including handling of petty cash, banking and audit procedures.

Funding allocations - how much do you or can you spend on equipment or printing of PR materials is dictated by the project needs/inputs and is often regulated by the donor's grant/loan rules. If your technical proposal to a donor includes a financial section then the funding allocation is probably by broader headings such as Staff Salaries, Materials and Equipment, etc. After you receive the funds then a more detailed budget, by specific line can be prepared.

Budget preparation is the task of the Finance Manager, which then gets approved by senior management or the Project Manager. Budgets are generally prepared quarterly, and often cover a full twelve months of activity, or the length of the project. Finance reporting/accounting is usually a monthly exercise and any changes identified in the monthly reporting are reflected in the remaining two months of the quarterly budget. Budget adjustments are common and regular and are a result of cash flow problems, late receipt of funds from the donor or delayed implementation of the project activities.

Forecasts are best prepared jointly by the finance and project staff, to ensure funds requested match the project targets. Forecasts are a management tool and can also be used to monitor progress…the actual expenditure against planned expenditure. Forecasts also assist donors who allocate funds to your organization/project in specified amounts and agreed upon times. Forecasting can be for any period of time, but most useful if it is on a quarterly basis.

Financial audits are generally a mandatory request from donors. These audits will include a review of financial procedures, cash receipts and payments plus office/project inventory inspections. Most donors would like to see audits conducted on a regular basis and will insist on a final year end or end of project audit.

Overall responsibility of these financial tasks falls on the shoulder of the Finance Manager, but who may have an accounts clerk, petty cashier or inventory person to assist him/her in carrying out the financial duties.

The Finance Manager reports and is responsible directly to the Director.

4.3.4 Criteria for a Finance Manager

This is usually the most difficult position to fill in any organization primarily because the Finance Manager has to be honest, trustworthy, able to maintain confidentiality, be firm in his/her actions, knowledgeable, creative and capable... In addition to being personable because the Finance Manager is often the first person, after the Director, contacted by counterparts, partners and donors.

4.3.5 What to look for when Hiring/Selecting a Finance Manager:

- ☑ Reputation and past work experiences... Get several references and check them out thoroughly.
- ☑ Knowledge of local tax laws, banking regulations, personnel and local labour practices.
- ☑ Knowledge of advanced banking computer software and understanding of accounting systems.
- ☑ Management and financial planning skills/ability... Many finance people are very good at operations, but not at fiscal planning...and you will need both skills.
- ☑ Past experience with financial reporting to governments/donors.

4.3.6 Setting-up a Financial Section within the Organization

The Director needs to be directly involved with the establishment of the financial department, the hiring of the financial staff and in the development of all banking and financial systems. Financial policies need to be developed to cover cash payments, check signing authority, procurement procedures, personnel (employee) agreements, equipment contracts, safety arrangements for the keeping of cash/check books, an understanding of who keeps the financial office/safe keys and lines of responsibility within the financial department i.e., what the petty cashier can or cannot do.

After determining the required personnel for both your administrative and project needs, please refer to other sections of this handbook for interviewing and hiring techniques. (Part Two, Chapter Three: Filling Human Resource Needs); tips on developing a Job Description and Performance Appraisals (Part One, Chapter Two: Performance Appraisals).

Project Management and Implementation

1
Project Management and Implementation Project Manager

Overview

Project management is a tough job. But just to make your life more *interesting* the development business has many different acronyms, phrases and terms for you to learn...and to deal with. We have included some of the common phrases and terms related to **Project Management** in the following paragraphs. We hope the definitions and explanations of these terms will help you to better understand, the development business and the management processes.

For the new Project Manager some of these terms may sound strange...for the more experienced Managers they are just a reminder. Regardless of your experience, you will need to develop a common understanding of these terms amongst your team, partners and others. This is essential for good programme communication.

1.1 Management Phrases

> ...Know these management phrases so that every one is speaking the same development language...

1. **Risk Assessment**... Really involves decision making, either by the team, as a group decision...or the Project Manager who takes the responsibility by him/herself and decides what to

do. Risk is always there in project implementation and it's difficult, if not impossible, to be able to say which direction is best. Risk often means the possibility of a financial loss, which may have implications to the organization, community and/or donor. Therefore, the Project Manager must be sure s/he keeps senior management abreast of the circumstances and potential risk situations.

2. **Contingency Planning**...is basically a 'back-up' plan to your original planning ideas and implementation steps. Contingency is not necessarily a revised plan, but a second option (or approach) to achieving your goals and objectives. You can also have contingencies in personnel and in financial budgets. You may wish to hire one particular individual, but perhaps s/he is not available...then you go to your contingency plan, or your second choice. In budgets contingencies are usually a percentage of the total budget that is held in reserve for use as and when needed.

3. **Stress Management**...is the art of *managing* work-related stress. Stress management programmes can include meditation, muscle relaxation exercises and training staff members to think more positively. The introduction of management techniques like good time management can also help reduce stress. Project Managers are often subject to stress and need to find the best solution for themselves and their staff to reduce anxiety and tension.

The same training and management techniques can help reduce *burn-out* as well, although burn-out can often be more easily resolved by changing the staff person's work schedule, position on the team (or transfer the person), or lessening the responsibilities and/or work load.

4. **Work spill over**...is a common problem in project management, especially in smaller organizations, where there is plenty of work and fewer people, often less qualified as well, to complete the work load. There are several ways to approach this problem.

- ☑ First, is to have the project Manager review the job description and tasks assigned to each employee to see if s/he is being assigned more than originally agreed to, and if there is a general increase in the number/complexity of tasks.
- ☑ Second, is to undertake a complete analysis to assess what the staff is being asked to do, by whom (government, partners, headquarters of the organization, etc.) and if indeed the right person has been assigned the appropriate tasks.
- ☑ Third, assess the number of staff available for the number of tasks being assigned or requested. It's advisable to undertake a good time management study and see how much time is wasted...on what and by whom.
- ☑ Fourth, the Project Manager can also take measures to reduce the number of visitors coming to the office, the amount of idle time on the internet, prioritize the attendance at meetings, identify poor office systems that consume and waste staff time and change them and introduce better work habits through staff training.

5. **Conflict Resolution**... Many experts believe the best way to resolve conflict is to share core values of the organization. This is a powerful mechanism that has often helped to resolve conflicts. However, even in an organization where core values are strong, there can be differences of opinions on how to handle issues/problems. In these instances, there is often an appropriate dispute resolution mechanism that will be found, because the core values are still present and people do find solutions.

Example: A grievance committee could be formed to resolve conflicts stemming from a disagreement during a performance review. Project Managers must be responsible for resolving conflicts.

6. **Strengths and Weaknesses**... Usually thought of as the first part of a swot Analysis (Strengths, Weaknesses, Opportunities, Threats)... Strengths are *positive things* and put you in a good (positive) position. Strengths can be skills (multi-lingual capabilities or specialization in IT), or perhaps having a solid organizational infrastructure for implementing projects. Weaknesses, on the other hand, are negatives and show *something* is lacking. Weaknesses can be linked to finances, but more often during the analysis, weaknesses are linked to an absence of qualified people to implement the project or poor leadership in managing the project needs.

7. **Visibility**... In this handbook visibility means promoting the image and informing general public on both the organization and its project activities. To generate or create this *visibility* a variety of media will be used. Selection of which media to use is often the biggest concern...and generally influenced by cost and coverage (ability to reach the intended target audience...or outreach). TV is considered as one of the most effective ways to reach the target group, but TV is also usually the most costly type of media. TV stations, like radio, break down their air time into *prime time* and *non-prime time*... Prime time being when most people are watching the television (listening to the radio)...and is more an expensive period of air time.

Determination of which media to use also depends on...

(i) Your target audience... (ii) When they watch/listen to the TV/radio...(iii) The length of your message (TV/radio spots are often only 10-20 seconds in length) and;...(iv) What information you wish to disseminate (are you trying to create an awareness ...or hoping to change behaviour).

Knowing the target audience...their current level of knowledge on the topic...their media habits (do they share newspapers amongst each other... If so, print media may be an option)...their preference for getting information (trust factor is important here... Some trust what they see, but not what they read)...and their literacy levels.

Any presentation has to be appropriate... Culturally sensitive as well as in context...attractive and eye-catching...inexpensive to design, print, produce and distribute ...informative in a language easily understood...easily distributed/stored...and creative and clever in getting the message across.

8. **New Change Language**... A concept being introduced by the World Bank, and some donors into the development jargon, but not fully accepted by the EU and others. Change language tries to redefine what is meant by *output, input, outcome,* etc...Far too complicated to begin describing in this handbook, but mentioned here so that you are aware of its existence. Bottom line... Know Your Donor!... And address your proposals accordingly to the *language* they are familiar with or are expecting to receive from you.

9. **Memorandum of Understanding (MoU)**... Please see glossary of terms and sample of MoU in the Annexes. This is basically a legally binding, contractual agreement between two parties who wish to associate or in some way work together. The MoU spells out exactly what each party promises to do and who is responsible for doing what.

10. **Terms of Reference (ToR)**... Please see the glossary of terms and the Annex for a sample of both the consultant's ToR and a ToR that covers the provision of services to be provided by the organization. Unlike an MoU, a ToR is not a contract/agreement, but rather a descriptive explanation providing background and information on the project needs and activities. Based on the ToR, the organization can prepare a technical proposal.

11. **Working with Beneficiaries**... Working with beneficiaries requires many things. Some of the important

requirements are: (i) Building trust and credibility on both sides... (ii) Ability to communicate, not only in the local spoken language, but in terms of *understanding* what each other is actually saying/meaning... (iii) Patience... (iv) Ability to correctly assess the needs...and not impose what the organization feels is the best... (v) Flexibility in implementation... (vi) Good, solid cultural understanding of the community...Formal and informal... (vii) Ability to accurately assess socio-economic conditions of the community... (viii) More patience.

12. **Working with Partners**...is often difficult...can be very time consuming...and is in today's development world a necessity in programme implementation. You work with good partners to improve programme implementation. Of course selection of the partner(s) is key... Be sure to choose a partner that is as committed to the project as you are... Has or can bring the skills that you/your organization cannot provide... Has a sincere interest in working with you... Has the resources available to undertake *their* portion of the project work. In a partnership it is always a good idea to determine at the beginning... Who is the boss!...and who, at the end of the project, has the responsibility for handing over the project and reporting of funds. This is generally covered in the MoU...where one organization is usually identified as the *lead* organization.

13. **Setting up Reporting Systems** (narrative and financial)... The organization, and often the donor too, will dictate when, and what type of reports are to be prepared and in what format. The idea of any report...narrative or written...is to keep those who are not in daily contact with the project activities aware, updated and informed on what is happening. The project Manager is generally responsible for preparing clear, concise and the timely submission of these reports.

Written Reports can go into more detail and perhaps provide samples of materials (brochures, posters, photos, etc.). **Narrative**

Reports will probably be time barred so the presenter will have to be very brief, but at the same time clear and concise. **Financial Reporting** and fiscal systems will generally be spelled out by the donor in any contract or in the MoU between the two parties. Financial systems should conform/comply to the local laws and regulations (taxes, social benefits) and be subject to **audit inspections. Internal Reports** often come in different styles. Some are memos providing information, instructions or report details...Others can be confidential. Private/personal matters should be covered in confidential internal reports only. Internal reports usually follow a format agreed upon by the organization and Managers. Internal reports, like field trips, can become historical documentation and are useful when preparing new proposals or in the review of *lessons learned.* Who writes internal reports and how they are to be circulated is a management policy decision.

14. **Reporting to the Donors** and keeping the donor informed is a key task of the Project Manager. Donors are busy people, so the reporting arrangements...the frequency, the content, the format...should be agreed upon at the beginning of the funding process. Donors generally want to know... How their money is being spent... Is it being spent on what they planned/agreed to support... Is it making an impact and are the beneficiaries happy/pleased... Is the project well monitored and implemented as per the agreed upon time schedule...and are the donors receiving recognition. Some donors are only interested in the accounting aspects of the project... How is the money being accounted for and by whom. In these cases make sure the finance person provides all details... Bank statements, pro-forma invoices properly approved, bid quotations from several firms, compliance to international standards, and any justification on expenditures that might seem unusual (not taking the lowest bid for example). Other donors are heavy on the economic side...And they prefer charts and grafts showing economic

impact, expenditure ratios and/or cost efficient systems being used. Photos are important... You can probably never send enough photos to the donor. Of course, if they have their face in the photos, their boss's face or an important visitor, it's even better. Donors will find out if *'things'* aren't going right ... So do not stretch the truth... Be forthcoming in your reporting. If there is a problem address how you plan to solve it... Not complaining, or going on endlessly about how difficult/unfair things are.

1.2 Management Tools

> ...Learn to use these management tools for improved programmes & project implementation...

1. **Monitoring and Evaluation (M&E)**...are both management tools ...and how you plan to monitor and evaluate the project should be clearly described in any proposal you send to donors. As the two functions are different, it is suggested that you list, and describe, each one separately in the proposal.

Monitoring

Basically, monitoring is the **tracking of progress** and measurement against planned achievements. Monitoring oversees the implementation of activities to see if actions are proceeding according to the plan. As a rule of thumb, but depending on the size and strengths of the field offices, it is suggested that monitoring activities be undertaken in-house by the project management staff.

Evaluation

The evaluation process generally **seeks answers**, as objectively as possible, on impact, effectiveness and efficiency in relationship to set objectives. Independent, outside evaluators are usually recommended, especially for the larger year end or final project evaluations, to bring *credibility* to the evaluation. The *findings* of the evaluation can be considered as **the benchmark or baseline**, which is the *starting point* for the next project intervention and/or activities.

2. **Indicators**...should be included in the log frame and are based on what the ToR indicates as the planned outcome. Indicators come in many shapes and sizes...but generally the donor is interested in measuring impact and performance... So the indicators you select should show (indicate) performance and impact. Indicators also need to be/should be verified by some evidence/proof...a government report, health records. [see section on Results Based Management RBM]. Some **examples** of indicators are as follows:

Expected Outcome	Indicator
New project design acceptable for funding.	Complete feasibility study on new project.
Reduced HIV infection in youth.	Prevalence among youth remains below X%.
Increased awareness of ECD in village X.	Ten newly trained CBD workers assigned.

Quick quiz:

Indicator # 1 above measures performance and indicator # 2 impact...What does # 3 measure? (Answer: Performance)

The data sources verifying indicator #1 can be the printed/published study of the survey findings; for indicator #2 data from the MoH statistics department records... Now what is the data source for indicator #3? (Answer: Employment contracts of the CBD workers).

3. **Methodology**...can be simply described as 'the way or how you will complete the project activities'. CBD is a methodology...ECD is another. Once you have decided what

methodology you will propose for undertaking the project activities, you must then describe *how* you and the organization will apply this methodology. Most donors will understand what ECD is... So you don't have to describe how ECD functions...but rather how the organization will manage various ECD activities...How the organization will collect the data on parents' knowledge about nutrition...or how you will introduce a pre-school curriculum into 'X' number of kindergartens. In your proposals the methodology will describe the *how*...plus the *what* and *when*.

4. **Budgeting**...is a key management tool and includes reporting to the auditors, maintaining correct records and reporting to tax officials, supplying accurate and complete documentation to the customs authorities, monitoring of expenditures, preparing budget forecasts and ensuring a smooth cash flow for project expenditures. The finance person is responsible for undertaking these tasks and is directly responsible to the Program Manager.

There is a wide selection of computer software packages that can help setting up the organization and project finance systems. Electronic systems are great...and don't forget to back them up. The organization's auditors should be requested to help, as a service, in the setting up of the accounting systems...and advise on what ledgers, inventory systems and banking procedures should be followed.

Donors will also often have their requirements on financial reporting procedures, so they should be contacted before finalizing the financial policies.

It is the organization's senior management, Project Manager and the Finance Manager who should set the finance policies on reporting, expenditure limitations/cut-offs, procurement and money movement within the organization/projects.

5. **Business Plans...** The organization's business plan is a management guide, highlighting a business–like approach in project implementation and leading towards an element of financial sustainability. The business plan should contain the programme's resources and services that could eventually provide some cost recovery. Also identify what resources will be available from the local organization staff to the partners, including the community. A business plan format has been included in the Annex of this handbook.

There are several different ways of putting a business plan together... But you should design your plan to benefit you...and then don't forget to use it. Share your plan with donors and partners as well... It's a planning tool for you, and a road map for them to follow. Some suggestions for preparing your business plans are given below:

Structure and Content of a Business Plan:

The following features should be addressed and included in a business plan:

- **Objectives**... What are the organization's primary objectives.
- **Resources**... What does the organization offer in terms of human and physical resources, and how do you plan to manage them.
- **Target Audience**... How do you plan to assist the beneficiaries in the target audience, what do you know about them, and what is the development strategy.
- **Finances**... What are the expected financial needs, what do you plan and forecast for future expenditures of the organization's development efforts.
- **Action plans**... Over the next twelve months what are the key steps that you plan to take in designing/developing your programmes and what is the time frame.

The business plan covers a twelve month period (usually from January to December...or the fiscal year of the government/donor) and must be revised on an annual basis. The business plan can contain the following income revenue generation concepts:

- Systems Development Techniques... Perhaps an MIS, procurement or computer system.
- Materials Development... Nutrition manuals, children's books can be produced and sold (affordably).
- Training and Capacity Building Services... Training of Trainers or peer education courses can be developed and become a source of revenue.
- Co-financing Development Components... The local organization can use individuals from its network to serve as paid consultants to communities, government ministries.

1.3 Income Generating Concepts

1. **Seed Grants**...are a good source of money, but can be very time consuming for the amount of money received. They serve an important function when introducing new concepts/ideas or when the organization is uncertain about working in a particular geographical or technical area. Seed grants can help build up the image and can extend the expertise of the organization...and they can also damage the organization if the projects fail miserably. The terms and conditions of the seed grant should be reviewed and discussed in detail before applying or accepting the money.

2. **Pilot Projects**...can be a source of small funding. Pilot projects are initiated to test the waters of a new concept or approach and to see if the concept/methodology will work. Pilots can be used to prove to certain donors/government officials that, indeed, the project is feasible. Sometimes pilots are started to gain experience and learn lessons from a *mini* undertaking before investing huge amounts of time and money

into a larger or countrywide effort. The reasons for implementing a pilot project are several:

- Provides a basis for larger funded projects.
- Removes uncertainty about the acceptance of the project.
- Can be implemented if there is a shortage of funds to undertake a larger scale project.
- Provides an opportunity to test the implementation methods and systems.
- To demonstrate a model for potential donors to evaluate and consider.

1.4 Specific Steps for New Programmes

Overview

This section is prepared primarily for new Project Managers who will need to set up field offices located outside the capital city. These new Managers will be responsible for project implementation, field office management, developing community participation, financial controls, donor solicitation, and reporting.

Many of you will be new at this type of operation and not familiar with everything that needs to be accomplished, thus the check lists on simple and routine matters. In addition, as capacity building of local expertise is important to the organization's future, some of the following paragraphs will address the roles and expectations of these new Managers. Of equal importance here, is to note some very critical changes in the structure of the field/branch office set-up...particularly staff and personnel needs, which should be adhered to by the new project Manager.

1.4.1 Functions and Roles of Programme Managers

New Team Members

As a newly appointed professional in this organization, responsible for setting up a field or branch office, there are certain expectations that senior management will have regarding your performance and your management style. Hopefully, a job description was given to you at the time of joining. If not, be sure to ask for one. However job descriptions can only go so far...and do not cover everything. Likewise, there is no training course in the world that can teach you how to become a loyal, dedicated believer in what you are doing...that must come from within. The very fact that you have been selected and are about to go into the field indicates that you have some qualities, separating you from the other candidates. Your *bosses* have confidence in your ability and believe you will do your best to accomplish the goals and objectives. We wish you the very best.

You have read in the other sections of this handbook about the importance your position as a Project Manager carries...and the responsibilities that have been placed on your shoulders. This is especially true with regard to implementation of the activities, the accountability of funds and the overseeing of others on your team. You are expected to be continually thinking about these responsibilities and conduct yourself in a professional manner at all times. Indeed, others will be around to support and assist, but the onus of disciplining yourself and motivating the team rests primarily on you.

Being a Manager is like being an older sister or father... You are expected to lead, guide, understand, sympathize and achieve. In the eyes of your colleagues you should be available to them 24/7 and the beneficiaries, whose quality of life you have accepted to improve, are depending on you, too. They will learn to rely on your judgement and depend on you very much for doing the right thing. Although the tasks will be challenging the rewards will be many... Enjoy and do well!

Your Role Within the Organization

As the new Project Manager, you wear several hats. At times, you will be a mentor...and other times a tormentor trying to get things done correctly and on time. You will carry the title of

Project Manager, but you will also be expected to get your hands dirty when the need arises. You will be in charge and responsible for everything and the glory…or blame…will be all yours. The achievements and accomplishments will depend largely on the decisions you make and how you manage your time and the skills of others. No one disagrees that the job can sometimes be difficult and thankless… But where else can you apply your skills and knowledge to serve for the betterment of the poor and needy.

You act as the eyes and ears of the organisation in the field. You have many skills and will no doubt learn much more during your time on these projects. You are expected to act responsibly and in the best interest of the organization. You will, to a great extent, be operating and managing your time independently…and it is for these reasons that you have been given this handbook. As the title says it's a guide, and is meant to assist you in the different tasks you have been assigned. The handbook does not have all the answers, but offers suggestions that you can draw on and hopefully help you find solutions.

In some sections the handbook offers tips on how to carry out your tasks…Other sections offer advice on how to set-up or establish certain procedures. All sections are important, because they all relate directly to project management. However, some hold a slightly higher importance…like working with donors and promoting the image of the organization. These sections impact greatly on the running and future of the organization. Some of the sections may not seem relevant at this stage in your assignment…but may prove useful later on.

1.5 Changes in the Staffing Structure - Roles and Responsibilities

So far, in this handbook we have viewed the staff in general terms…primarily to demonstrate to donors what type of permanent employees the organization will need to support and implement the projects. With the introduction of a field or branch office, there will also be a shift in staffing or personnel needs. Many of the positions to be filled will be temporary or for a specific task only. The roles of the 'field or branch office' personnel will usually be more technical or activity specific, with administrative functions either handled by the project Manager directly, or with support links from the main office. Those working for/in the *main* organization have a more or less permanent status, while those assigned directly to project activities are in a time-barred situation, and therefore, somewhat less permanent. The differences between organization and project are made primarily to reflect the options in office arrangements and staffing patterns, as indicated below.

The following suggestions are given to provide for maximum cost efficiency, and should be adapted to local conditions and the changing organizational management needs. Management is not an exact science...(Refer Part II, Chapter 4 for detailed staffing structures).

Identifying the Differences between Organization and Project Staff

Having field/branch offices is always a tough situation...and can cause some tense moments for people in both offices. Roles and responsibilities must be well defined so that everyone knows their function. Ideally the main office is to support...administratively and technically as asked. The field office is where the projects are actually managed and implemented... But it's not a perfect world, so problems will arise. Most *hiccups* occur when there is a difference in management approaches, or with reporting (lack of, usually), and at times, the quality of work, including the meeting of deadlines.

In principle, the (headquarters) main office functions primarily as an administrative support office, with PERHAPS some indirect project supervision responsibilities. If this is the case the *indirect* project responsibility must be clearly defined. The management and implementation of the technical projects is generally left to the field or branch office. They are located where the work is going on, where the activities are being carried out and exposed to the barriers and problems. Of course, sorting out these *lines* of functions can prove confusing at times, especially when it's time for decision making on key issues...or defining *who is in charge* of project and running the show. Good communication between all parties is necessary here.

As the field or branch office is responsible for implementation and management of the project details, the project management should be carried out by the field the Project Manager and his/her staff. Of course, there will be certain financial and administrative duties as well, supported hopefully, by the main office.

2

Steps to Programme and Project Implementation

Overview

So now you have the funding, the project agreements/contracts have been signed with the donor and government...Now what do you do? Well, after all the hard work and bull fuzz of proposal writing and contract negotiating, it's time to implement the project...and this should be the fun and exciting part.

Now is a good time to review your technical proposal...Look at the methodology, time lines and other implementation steps...and then get moving... Usually start dates are delayed, but donors/governments like to keep the project completion times as per their original plans... Good Luck!

Part 1 of this handbook covered management terms and phrases, and provided some tips and tools for new Managers. In Part 2 it will be assumed the organization is set up and running and will, therefore, focus on the **implementation** of the programme and project activities.

In this part, we will discuss the management and leadership aspects necessary to successfully implement the projects, address the steps required for undertaking and completing the planned project approach and identify how the implementation process is and should be monitored, including various evaluations.

Project implementation may be of a totally new project, or the 2nd or 3rd phase of an ongoing project...... or the implementation of the pilot project' we discussed earlier.

2.1 Pre-Project Implementation

2.1.1 Situation Analysis

A situation analysis (needs assessment) is necessary to avoid 'the garbage in - garbage out' syndrome. Research establishes the benchmark/baseline for identifying the needs (also can help in preparing the problem statement). To start a project with insufficient or unreliable data will produce a failure. When you initiate your situation analysis:

PLEASE REMEMBER TO
Use a professional team, preferably local, to design, undertake, and analyze survey instruments and data.
Use statisticians for drawing the sampling size and type of sampling method to be used (random, stratified or??).
Use a social scientist (sociologist) to design the questionnaires/survey instruments, do the questionnaire pre-testing and conduct the Focus Groups Discussions (FDGs).

You need to have the social scientist and economist to undertake the analysis. When the analysis is complete it is a good idea to share the research findings with donors, government counterparts. Always build your projects based on the findings...in other words...use the data collected for designing and monitoring your projects.

Example of a Situation Analysis

Programme Background... There was an established local organization, using donor funds, and in operation for more than five years. The organization wished to expand its operations and seek additional funding.

Situation Analysis... The organization undertook a situation analysis using a series of one-on-one interviews... Asking donors, private pharmacists and government officials about their intention/ability to procure and distribute modern contraceptives. The responses (data and findings) were then analyzed by an economist and demographer, resulting in the following analysis of the contraceptive situation.

Conclusion...Based on this situation analysis the organization is now prepared to write a technical proposal requesting additional funds for contraceptive supply and also for distribution and promotion costs.

The situation analysis determined that:

- The public health sector cannot fill the contraceptive product needs/demands, especially in the rural areas.
- The private sector is still unable to provide high quality, affordable products on a regular basis. The market structure is in place, but continuous supply/import remains irregular.
- Awareness of modern contraceptive methods is strong in the urban areas, but still remains weak in the rural areas.
- Contraceptive prevalence is still low at less than 20 %, abortions are less common than they were five years ago, but are still performed, many still in unsafe conditions.
- HIV infection rates are increasing annually in general population and research indicates that intravenous drug use is on the rise, especially amongst the vulnerable groups.

Social Research

Social Research is complex and complicated...and can cover a wide range of things – Social values, social norms, social relationships, institutions, attitudes, opinions, behaviour's and should only be undertaken by a professional...preferably a sociologist or other social scientists, or a validated organization. Social Research implies a complex methodology requiring professional expertise. The methodology refers to sampling, problem identification, data collection, analysis including statistical and content analysis, among others.

Social Research is one of the first steps in building/implementing a programme and required for the collection of data, which is to be analyzed for problem identification and find possible solutions. Social Research is also used to prepare baselines for future evaluations. There are methods and techniques for undertaking social research that are used to survey the social phenomenon/ problems. They can be grouped into two main categories - quantitative and qualitative. Under quantitative you have closed end questionnaires (structured questionnaires), which is the main one and also interviews, with an accompanying questionnaire. Qualitative includes Focus Group Discussions (FGD), in-depth interviews (non-structured), case studies, brainstorming, Delphi, group discussions and Participatory Research Action (PRA).

Research is to *search* for something... It requires the design of a questionnaire, a decision on the type of methods and techniques to be used and how you collect, analyze and interpret the data and findings. In other words, the methodology of Social Research represents an algorithm of steps or components of research, which include:

- documentation/desk review (what is known about that particular problem/phenomenon). This is known as Problem Identification.
- definition of the problem, theoretical, operational, hypothesis, dimensions and variables of the problem.
- construction of the sample (size of the population to be included in the Social Research, for example).
- the choice of methods and techniques most applicable/adequate to that social problem you are studying.
- data Collection.
- statistical Analysis.
- report Writing.

The objectives of the study, based on your hypothesis, will determine what type of methodology you use... Do you use quantitative...qualitative...or both? Selection of the methodology is always influenced by costs.

Quantitative studies are more expensive, but are realistic and validity is higher. It is often recommended that researchers use qualitative methods...such as focus groups to find a trend, which can be elements for your hypothesis. Then you can use the data from these FGDs for operationalizing your questionnaire.

One of the first steps in Social Research is to identify and list the social problems which impact the group you are targeting. A common sense definition of a social problem:

A Social Problem is...
A problem that happens to a statistically significant/representative number of people with serious consequences for that particular group.

To assist in Problem Identification a 'Problem Tree', which will provide a logical analysis, is included in the Annex of this manual. Some pointers on how and what this Problem Tree represents is provided below:

The Problem Tree is divided into three basic parts:

- Root Causes (fundamental)
- Underlying Causes
- Manifestations (of the problems or phenomena)...

And are categorized as follows:

1) Root causes could be...

- Unequal distribution of economic and developmental resources.
- Fluctuating economic growth that hinders human development.
- Political instability and lack of democratic culture.
- A strongly stratified society/social structure with severe inequality.
- Unequal distribution of wealth and power.
- Geographical disparity in terms of social and cultural modernization.

- The secular norms, attitudes and practices vary significantly amongst different regions.
- Social mobility is not fuelled only by education.

2) Underlying causes...

- Social policies are not effective and efficient.
- Provision of social services, including basic services is limited.
- Level of public expenditure on education, health social protection is low.
- Performance of the organizational management is low.
- *Culture* to operate in organized, well managed situations is low.
- Decentralization of the decision making process is still slow and hasn't yet reached the community level.
- Monitoring and evaluation systems are not in place.
- Capacity building of the systems and the strengthening of professional capabilities for development of human resources are inadequate.

3) Manifestations...

- Access to basic services are considerably limited for children, including adolescents, and parents.

The smart Project Manager will *manage* the intervention on his/her own and NOT do the research. Untrained/unskilled (in the field of social research) Project Managers should:

1. Help in identifying the problem.
2. See what information/data is already available on the problem (studies/reports).
3. Determine what research is necessary.
4. Check best resources to undertake the research.
5. Develop a good ToR for the research.
6. Launch a research bid.
7. Select the research organization.
8. Supervise strict adherence to the ToR.
9. After research findings are received organize consultative workshop of researchers to validate the report.

10. Use the evidence based knowledge to design a social policy.

To undertake social research without proper expertise is dangerous...You may reach wrong conclusions, provide wrong solutions. To understand the complexity of Social Research Methodology, please *Google* social research methodologies, and look at the variety and detail available.

Example of Social Research

The Social Research method applied was a household study using a questionnaire, with some open ended questions based on a random sample to see the impact of HIV/AIDS on families. The response to the HIV/AIDS questionnaire was at the household level. The impact of the epidemic on families and households evolve over time, and each household possesses its own constraints and opportunities for coping. The ability to cope with HIV/AIDS and mitigate its impact, however, depends largely on the household's initial economic and social resource base and its capacity to stabilize or increase income.

Whereas relatively wealthy households are likely to shift their budget allocations, poor households with fewer assets often adopt coping mechanisms that are irreversible and affect the survival of the family members left behind. Thus, by definition, the poorest are least able to cope with the effects of HIV/AIDS, and are rendered more insecure and vulnerable in the long-term.

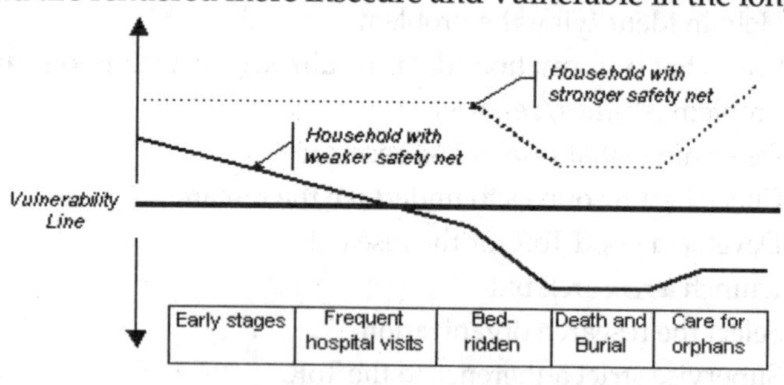

Source: CARE's SIMBA Project – Evaluation Report

In order to cope with the loss of adults, households and extended families often reallocate their resources and turn to friends and relatives for cash and other kinds of assistance. Poorer households, having fewer assets, are likely to have more difficulty in coping as compared to those with more assets.

Analysis I

This analysis is looking at the findings of the survey and coming to some conclusions, based on the information/data collected. The findings are what you need to analyze. If the survey/study is done correctly and completely...then the analysis of the findings will provide you with the facts and figures you need to make decisions for project implementation...or indicate where there are gaps and indicate where additional information is required; the findings will provide you with the information you need about the community's needs... Perhaps even provide some insight into what inputs/contributions you can plan to receive from the community

Analysis II

Before undertaking a new survey or study be sure to see if there is a study already completed or being planned by someone else; assess the usefulness of undertaking a rapid assessment study or doing a swot Analysis instead of a major research study to collect the data you require.

2.2 Beginning to Implement the Projects

Overview

In your project proposal, you prepared plans, timetables, and steps on how to implement the project. Most probably, some length of time has passed from the date you submitted your proposal until it was approved or funds made available for implementation. There is also a chance that the community or others have begun some activities in the proposed area. Therefore, the first thing you should do is undertake a review of the current situation and **revise the work plan accordingly.**

2.2.1. Work Plan Revision

This task should be transparent, undertaken in collaboration with the government officials involved in the project, the community, and other project partners. The work plan and activities should not deviate from the original proposal, but rather update the situation/events. Key in the revision is the revised time line, indicating when the activities are to be started and completed and any changes, if there are, in the implementation steps and/or procedures.

Some points to consider when revising the work plan

- Often, considerable time has lapsed between the original proposal submission and the receipt of funding... So revise the plans accordingly, but after meetings/visits as described in the next point.
- Plan official introductory meetings ... For yourself and other senior staff on programme activities...with government officials, partners and others involved with programme implementation.
- Organize joint field visits to programme areas with partners to... Check data, note any changes in programme needs, identify any obstacle, understand the current status fully.
- Identify personnel and equipment needs... Refine budgets, per diems and travel schedules, based on current conditions (increased petrol costs, hotel rates, etc.)
- After visits and meetings, revise the work plan and submit in a draft form to the counterpart/donor (review requirements based on the signed agreements).
- Prepare an 'action plan', usually covering detailed activities for a period between six – twelve months. Once the action plan is prepared/approved, it is a good time to assign tasks to the project personnel responsible for implementation. (See section on Job Descriptions).
- Organize a workshop/seminar/meeting to introduce your programme and seek the support of others who may be involved in your programme.

2.2.2. Set-up Management and Monitoring Systems

- Management Systems would include a computerized MIS, financial disbursement procedures, and office operations for implementing the activities.
- Monitoring Systems would include establishing indicators (both performance and impact indicators), identifying who will be in-charge of monitoring and reporting systems.
- Once Management and Monitoring Systems are developed by the Programme Manager who should also prepare 'Programme Policies' that would cover office operations, personnel as well as programme activities.
- Use your log frame, from the proposal, for monitoring.

2.2.3. Identify Barriers

- An ongoing process…and once identified be sure to try and *solve* only those that you have some control over…natural disasters, revolutions are out of your control.
- Anticipate needs… Often barriers come up because the programme did not look far enough down the road to anticipate possible barriers (increased taxation, changes in government policy).

2.2.4. Evaluations

- Timings and types of the evaluation are usually based on what you describe in your proposal. (Check log frame).
- Make sure you have an accurate benchmark (starting point) on which to base your evaluation. Benchmark data should be reliable.
- Determine what you are measuring (evaluating)…performance, change in behaviour, impact (on health) or…???
- Properly identify who is responsible for undertaking the evaluation and when they will be conducted. Often an external evaluator is needed.
- Joint evaluations with government/partners show great transparency.

- Organize a workshop to present the evaluation findings. If you have a lengthy evaluation, for more than two months, it is nice to prepare a half-day session with your 'interim' findings...to keep people informed/updated.

As A Reminder, Be Sure to do the Following:

Consultative Workshops... After the work plans have been revised, and approved by the government/donor if necessary, it is always a good idea to organize a half or one day workshop/seminar to introduce the new plans. This will keep everyone informed and increase the ownership aspects of the project. The workshop should be held in an accessible location for maximum participation and at a convenient time for key actors/players to attend.

Prepare Action Plans... This planning process will redefine the project goals, re-establish the steps for implementation, assist the Project Manager in the execution of project activities, identify project resource needs and establish set points for monitoring. Action plans will also provide the baseline data, or starting point of the project, which is necessary for the evaluations.

Procurement of Resource Needs... The action plans have identified the resource needs...and now is the correct time to purchase the new equipment (additional computers, desks, vehicles, etc.) and to set up appropriate inventory systems. Procurement guidelines of the donor or the organization should be checked and complied with.

Project Staffing... Also after finalization of the action plans it is the right time to hire the project staff. The revised work plan/time line will indicate when the various personnel should join and what their responsibilities will be. Once the interviews have been held and personnel selected then job descriptions should be issued.

Project Implementation... You have the equipment set up, the new staff members have been hired and you have the activities and tasks identified... Now you are ready for implementing the activities. Implementation of the activities will be as described in the revised work plans and monitored by the assigned project staff.

Financial Management... The setting up of Financial Accounting and Reporting Systems is a critical and first step in Programme Implementation. Guidelines for fiscal control will come from the organization or the donor...or both. Account records, including banking procedures, must be maintained to strict audit regulations. Funds, if kept in the office must be secured. Disbursement and receipt of funds should be according to the organizational policies.

Monitoring... of the project inputs and activities is one of the main responsibilities of the Project Manager or his/her designated Project Officer. Monitoring, a continuous, ongoing process, is the tracking of progress or impact and informs the management if there is discrepancy or deviation from the planned activities. Based on the monitoring results, corrections or changes are made to the plan.

Evaluations...are a more scheduled event that occur at set times during project implementation. Evaluations focus more on specific questions related to effectiveness and impact. The findings from the evaluations are often the basis for making changes in future programmes or project activities.

Report Writing... It is the responsibility of every Project Manager to report on the progress, problems and achievements of the project. Reporting could be on a monthly, quarterly or at other agreed upon times. The organization as well as the donor may have specific report writing format requirements. Photos usually make a nice addition to quarterly or annual reports.

Closing down a project... Phasing out, turning over, or closing down is part of project implementation, and is covered in Part III, Chapter 3 of this handbook.

3

Financial Planning

3.1 Budget Forecasting

This is a task to be completed by the Finance Manager, and reviewed/approved by the Manager/Director. Forecasts are a planning tool and also useful for financial monitoring... Forecasts should be prepared prior to the time period where the funds will be required. Many forecasts are prepared quarterly and can serve as a basis for funding requests from the main office (headquarters) or the donor. Others may prefer an annual budget forecast, broken down by quarters, which can be reviewed by the organization's Board of Directors/donors for an overview of how the funds will be allocated during the coming year. Forecasts cover all line items in the budget (operations/equipment, etc.) and footnotes explaining unusual amounts, plus any advance of funds should be included.

3.2 Fund Raising

Identifying donors and locating sources of funding is a major role of the organization's Manager/Director, but fund raising is everyone's responsibility...and to everyone's benefit. In other sections we have discussed possible sources of funding...DFID, USAID, Private donors (Bill Gates Foundation, International NGOs, etc.). However, in this section we would like to provide some ideas on how to possibly *attract donors*.

1. **Visibility (PR) Materials**... Good, professionally prepared materials (brochures, power point presentations) is an effective way to attract donors, the materials should be complete...and describe clearly the activities, costs,

personnel needs. Visibility materials need to be easy to read, concise and prepared in appropriate language.

2. **Pilot Projects**... Another way to demonstrate your organization's capabilities to donors is through the implementation of pilot projects. These *"show pieces"* provide donors the opportunity to actually see how the project is implemented, what is needed (equipment/personnel) and will, hopefully provide some positive end results.
3. **Concept Papers**...are a short version of a proposal. They are a brief, but detailed description of an idea (concept) which, if properly funded can become a much larger project. Concept papers provide an overview of how the project will be implemented, and include the costs involved, and expected outcomes.
4. **Seed Grants**... Some donors still offer *seed* money for introducing new concepts/ideas or for the funding of pilot projects. Seed grants like other donor money, has its specific terms and conditions... But more often than not seed money generally requires some assurance, by the donor, that additional or continuing funding is in the pipeline. Seed money is to basically 'get you started'...and not for long term project activities.
5. **Matching Grants**... Matching grants or matching funds are a financial mechanism available from many donors. Matching grants is quite different from the *co-financing* mechanism also available from many donors for covering project costs. Please be careful not to confuse the two. Matching grants have no standard provisions and each grant is handled on a separate basis. Donor participation in matching grants will usually vary from the type of project activities they are willing to fund, to the amounts/limits of the match...often expressed in percentage. The rule of

thumb is...matching grants are negotiable and your best negotiating skills will be required to get the best deal.

It is also, generally accepted, that an NGO can use a percentage of its running costs against the match. Most NGOs find a way to reduce the actual cash required for the match to as little as possible. In some cases, such as disaster relief or emergency programmes, NGOs have probably raised funds for the disaster/emergency from other sources and have no problem adding the donor funds to cover the match.

Unusual example:

This creative matching grant took place in Haiti. The Government of Haiti was required to provide a certain percentage of funding to complete a safe drinking water project. The Government was unable to meet their match. The NGO then suggested to the donor, USAID, that the government's share of the match could be met by putting a *dollar* value on the water being extracted from the ground...the donor accepted. In other words...monetary value can be placed on non-monetary inputs if you can get the donor to agree.

The European Union has a format (under TACIS) for matching grants, with their usual conditions attached when applying for such funding. Additional information can be found in their website: ec.europa.eu/comm/europeaid/ cgi/frame12.pl

3.3 Know Your Donor

Know your donor's primary programme focus and/or interest. We are sure that everyone is aware of this suggestion, and also that you realize your purposed donor won't consider funding a family planning activity if they are focused on funding agricultural projects. However, did you consider knowing or finding out from the donor the following points?

QUESTIONS TO ASK DONORS		
1.	What is the maximum amount of money the donor will provide?	For a specific project/ component.
		For how many years/months or, for how many project phases will they provide funding?
		Is there a clause that says you must spend 'X'amount of your own funds before 'Y'will be allocated by the donor.
2.	What are the strings attached?	The project must buy equipment from a certain country.
		Donor can only fund a "part" of an activity (educational materials, but not commodities).
		Cannot fund full range of programme needs, only a certain segment in partnership with other donors/government.
		Does your programme have to be a part of a national programme or linked to the government?
		Is there a cap on funding levels?
		Is funding contingent on certain laws being passed, or the organization achieving a certain level of sustainability.
3.	What are the reporting requirements?	Reports prepared in what language.
		In what format.
		What is the reporting period?
		Is the reporting on financial aspects only or both activity progress and expenditures?
		What should the report highlight (number of beneficiaries, geographical outreach)?

	Do they want to see a specific link between their funding input and the achievements of that segment, or do they want an overview of the complete programme implementation progress?
4. Who are the key officers/decision makers in the funding organization?	What are his/her pet interests, dislikes, attitudes towards the programme on focus?
	How does s/he measure *success* of a project?
	Are they supportive?
	What are the donor's impressions of the country in general, does your programme fit into the overall interests (development or political) of the donor?

3.4 Selling Your Organization and Projects

How you sell your organization and programmes will depend a lot on the answer you receive from the donor's questions above (3.3)? You will also have to give some thought on what types of materials you will develop and print about your project/organization, both for donor use and general public. Dissemination of information, projecting a positive image of your organization and explaining what expertise you can provide is an ongoing activity. The following are some tips that may be useful in promoting your project and organization:

- Sell your programme by providing the donor with informal **news or milestones** of your achievements... Don't wait for the official reporting period. A short note with a new brochure is always appreciated.
- Follow the KISS system when writing promotional materials... **Keep It Short and Simple**! Donors don't have a lot of time to read, but **they want to be informed**; write in a language people will understand by avoiding a lot of

acronyms, also remember they may be reading your materials in a language other than their mother tongue.

- **Write in terms they understand**. If the decision maker/responsible person in a donor organization is a medical doctor, then highlight and include medical terms - TFR or CPR figures... If an economist then provide statistics/graphs and if you have to satisfy both then provide a chart that shows your programme having influence or impact on the TFR.
- Indicate in your materials (formal or informal) any visits by the donor to your project and also **illustrate the management and monitoring systems** that you have in place. Monitoring, in addition to evaluations, is becoming more of an interest to donors, especially as they track long range activities. **Remember: the people want to know what you have done with their money... what are the results**! They would like to know where and how the funds were spent, and of course, an accounting of the funds.
- Bring out in your materials visits by the partnerships you have formed (with NGOs, private sector and/or government) and how you practice/implement **good resource utilization and harmonization**. Cost sharing is a key buzz word as well.
- The E and E twins **(efficiency and effectiveness**) are always important to people. You must show efficiency - systems used and/or goals reached as per your action plan). And effectiveness - the management structure employed by your organization. **Show how you have avoided duplication of efforts of other donors/programmes.**
- Know how to present your project... **Use the right people to give presentations,** focus on donor interests, keep the *bull* down to a minimum as people will cross check your records/statements, and don't be embarrassed if you don't achieve your goals... It isn't a perfect world, but you should show where the lapses are and *the lessons learned* from the experiences. **Show steps you will take for improving**, and

these steps should be concrete/workable and spelled out clearly.

- **Demonstrate your knowledge** of what other international donors/bodies/NGOs are doing in the same sector and overall, what funding levels are being provided to the sector you will be working in. Indicate what the **government commitment** is to in the long range goal of your programme. This is best stated in laws, regulations and policies presented by the government.
- **Be honest** with the people, tell them first because they will find out anyway... It is a small world and a close community. They are also aware that *things* happen and **there will be problems**. When describing a failure or less than expected result be sure to put a positive spin on it by showing how you have corrected the problems and how you will prevent this from happening again by expressing systems that have been developed or checks and balances put in place.
- **Sustainability**... It won't go away, so work on it, show the donor how you are achieving it, and include ways of reaching sustainability in your proposals.

3.5 Donors and Partnerships

WHAT is a donor...WHO is a partner...WHAT constitutes a Stakeholder?

Donors... Usually provide cash funding, through grants or loans to the country programme and/or directly to a project activity. Donors can also offer contributions in kind (equipment, office space, vehicles) or provide free of charge technical assistance (TA)... who are most often experts in the technical field/skill area. Grants do not need to be paid back to the donor... Loans usually do. Both financial instruments have rules and regulations that must be followed when accepting the funds...This will include accountability of the money, and guidelines on how and for what the funds may be spent. Failure to spend the funds to the donor's requirements could result in losing the funding or legal action if misuse is evident. Long term grants/loans will generally have an external audit requirement. If a contribution of equipment or a vehicle is provided, there are usually rules and guidelines that must be followed for procurement, vehicle use and upkeep...including how to dispose of the equipment/vehicle when the project is completed.

Donors...can be host country governments, usually specific departments within the Ministry, international or branch offices of organizations (Rotary, Lions Club), development sections of governments (DFID, SIDA, USAID, KfW), individual foundations (Packard, Gates, Aga Khan), religious organizations (Islamic fund, CRS), corporations (Coke Cola, Adidas, Ford Motor Company), UN organizations (UNICEF, UNFPA, UNDP), international development organizations (World Bank, Asian Development Bank, Islamic Development Bank) and international NGOs (CARE, Plan International, Save the Children). Each donor has a different project support focus/interest, different funding levels, a different set of guidelines on fund allocation, different reporting systems/requirements, different donor identification (perhaps their logo on brochures, sign boards)...But ALL donors will require you to submit a written proposal or concept paper for the funds/contributions that you are requesting. Most of the donors will have their own application format and information requirements.

Donors...can also be partners. While many donors, like UNICEF or USAID, are considered to be *non-operational* partners (they are present in country, but do not actually implement projects... Instead they provide funding or joint funding for someone else to implement) they are still considered a partner. In other cases there are partners who provide funding/expertise, but who also participate in project design, planning and implementation...often referred to as a working or consortium partners. Usually these partners are international NGOs, international organizations and consulting firms.

Partners...can be from one or more organizations...can even be the host government. Partners can be *silent*, those who are not involved with any aspect of the implementation and who do not require any recognition for their support/ contribution...or the more traditional partner...where the group(s) join together in *implementing* the project in a *working partner* relationship, with each organization (partner) providing their specific skill/knowledge for the good of the project. Community Based Development Projects often consider the community, leaders as a partner, with the community as a whole, the *stakeholders*, or people who will benefit from the outputs/outcomes of the programme interventions.

There are several good reasons to have partners assisting or a part of the organization...and not only for financial reasons. The partnership could assist:

- With human resource sharing.
- Provide office or storage space.
- Extend or leverage the resources of the new organization's projects.
- Or eventually be the recipient of the phasing out from a larger project when the international organization departs from the country.

Stakeholders... In UN *speak* stakeholders are known as *duty bearers*. Stakeholders are also often involved with the decision making aspects of the project and the implementation methods. One big difference is stakeholders can indirectly benefit, or be the recipients of the project inputs.

An Example:

In building a new school the students (beneficiaries) benefit directly with the new facility, and the stakeholders, who are the local authority, school administration and teachers will benefit indirectly as a result of the new school.

Organizations... All development organizations require donors to fund their operations (administrative support) and projects. The relationship with the donor is often purely financial, as most large donors are non-operational. Organizations generally sign a working agreement (MoU) with partners who participate in project implementation. It is a good idea for an organization to have a link, perhaps even a formal tie up or partnership, with the host country government. Donors like to see government involvement and participation.

Projects... All projects will require donor funding and should have partners, including the government as appropriate, for project implementation... The reasons for having partners include:

- Improved technical ability.
- Increased financial contributions.
- Expansion of geographical areas (urban/rural).
- Extended time frames (length of project activity);
- Sustainability.

3.6 Phasing out the Project

Phasing out and closing down a project activity might be necessary. All good things must *sometimes* come to an end...and you should be well aware of what to do when it happens. In some situations the projects may be forced to close down... Due to civil disturbances or events beyond control of the organization or Project Manager. In other instances there is a planned and managed turning-over or phasing-out of project activities as a result of the project being completed, additional funding was not available or nationalization of the project.

To protect the organization and its assets from a sudden or unforeseen closure a 'force majeure' clause should be inserted in the MoU. This is a standard protection clause found in most contracts and can be prepared by your legal advisor.

A Manager/Director may experience different types of project slow downs or organization closings. The following are some illustrative examples of what might happen and how the Manager/Director can be prepared.

- **Complete phase out**... This should be a planned phasing out process conducted in a gradual, step-by-step way. The phasing out details should have been included in the original programme document/proposal and if donor money is involved they should be made aware of what is happening. Complete phase out requires turning over of all tasks, responsibilities, materials and equipment to, either, the community, government, or returned to the donor (according to the original agreements). Receipts for equipment/materials may be required by auditors/ donors. Hopefully the phasing out doesn't mean the end of the activity, but instead has been turned over to the local community or integrated into the government's programme...in which case a phasing out ceremony, with great fanfare, should be organized.
- **Gap between projects**...Gaps between phases of projects, due to lack of funding, personnel and/or other resources is not uncommon...and should be anticipated in your Log Frame (under possible barriers/obstacles). Filling the gap is not always easy. Sometimes existing personnel can be re-assigned to other project activities...or sent to other countries. If they are very good and you if you want them to come back... Then perhaps they can be put on temporary leave at a reduced salary. Good monitoring will often give the Manager/Director or project staff sufficient warning that problems are ahead and a break (gap) in the activities can be expected. Gap identification should be accounted for when you are preparing the 'Problem Statement' in the original proposal,

and can be somewhat *cushioned* by including a contingency fund in the project budget.

- **Handing over the work to another organization**...can be a part of your sustainability measure...or a last minute effort to save the project since you can no longer support the activities. Handing over a project administratively is somewhat like a complete phase out (see above for requirements). Ideally, if you plan to hand over a project or project activity, then this should be done in a gradual way, to allow for the new organization/group to be well trained and to properly assume responsibilities. Handing over is a lot like delegation... You relinquish authority to others, hand over the tasks completely and can no longer be involved with the events.
- **Departing from the specific sector**...Departing from a sector activity is a major programme decision and should be based on some logical explanation. There can be some legitimate reasons for such departures... Change in government strategies, there is no longer a need, or too many other players/actors have become involved in this sector and your organization can no longer make an impact. If you have been in this sector for a long time and then decide to depart be prepared to perhaps answer some questions from government officials and/or donors as to why you are leaving.

Summary on phasing out:

In case of a planned phasing-out or project closing, it is suggested to try and work as closely with the beneficiaries/ stakeholders, before your organization's involvement is stopped completely. This will ensure maximum continuity of the project and protect your past investment.

At the time of closing, a thorough review of the past project activities should be undertaken, to acquire the *lessons learned* for future use and planning. A project evaluation should be conducted, to help point out what worked...what didn't work...and why.

It is also quite common, especially from the donor's side, to ask the programme people to prepare a final report on the closing out of the project. This report, which will cover the past accomplishments, results, highlights (systems installed, training conducted), failures, problems, reasons for closure, expenditures, disposition of materials and equipment, any legal issues resolved/pending and the next step forward. All good things must come to an end...including your programme activities. Your original proposal will cover the phasing out of the activities, and give the approximate timings of closing and what you will have/hope to have achieved before you turn off the lights. Hopefully, the technical design in your proposal will include training, capacity building for another entity or the community to take over...and carry on the initial activities you have introduced/started.

In order to ensure an orderly exit...and continuation of the activities...the Manager/Director, will, from day one, have to be cognizant of the need to develop exit strategies. These strategies should be easily followed by those who will take over.

Exit Strategies:

- Exit plans must be discussed well in advance with government and/ or partners...and have their approval before you begin to phase out an activity.
- Target groups/beneficiaries and the government must be informed from the very beginning that the funding is limited, and programme activities are time barred. They should be advised that eventually 'they' will have to assume the project tasks/activities.
- Strategies must be developed during the implementation period and set in such a way that local people...in the absence of your team...can implement or maintain the project. A balance between available resources... Use of technology...and skill levels of those taking over must be assessed by your team before closing down.

- A review of the original programme contract should be made to ensure that your organization has satisfied the conditions of the contract...both in terms of financial expenditures and goals achieved. Signed documents, between staff and the new entity, should be prepared covering the handing over and receipt of all materials, equipment, files, etc.
- A phasing out workshop, to ensure transparency and better ownership, is often a nice way to prevent any possible problems after your organization departs.

Steps for Exiting:

- At a minimum, six months before your organization leaves the project, the phasing out/exit plans should begin.
- The phasing out should be completed in a systematic way, turning over all aspects of the programme one by one as the new entity/community can manage to undertake these tasks.
- Your team should be available to observe the programme under the *new* programme management for a specified period of time before departing completely.
- It is the responsibility of the Manager/Director to properly train, and evaluate the skills/capabilities of the *new* management before signing off on each of the programme components.
- The *new* management team should have a thorough knowledge and understanding of the programme goals and objectives.
- Planning is probably the weakest part of any new entity's 'taking over' of a programme. Your team shouensure that programme plans/activities/time lines are given to the new management team and there is a clear understanding of these plans.

The end

And hopefully a new beginning for a: "properly dressed manager"!

Annexe 1

Work Plan Model

Annual Work Plan for: Early Childhood Development

Annual Project Objectives: **Total: $ 65 000**	(1) All (or give a % or number) children from birth to age 7 are provided with proper care and support for their intellectual, physical, cognitive, social and emotional development by their families and communities. (2) The child's optimal development and learning processes are supported and stimulated in a 'friendly and enabling environment' in the home and in all childcare settings.						
Year:	2006						
Programme Cycle:	1 year						
ACTIVITY DESCRIPTION	PLANNED OUTPUT	TIME FRAME	PLANNED AMOUNT	*PBA (s)*	*RESERV ATION*	PARTNER (s)	RESPONSIBL E PERSON

SUB: PROJECT DESCRIPTION: **Capacity Building**						OBJECTIVES: - The local governments and communities are supported in establishing quality community-based child-care services. - Preschool workers have capacity to provide ongoing support to families and create learning and stimulation environment at preschool establishments. - Community leaders mobilize resources and activate people to get involved in the children's well-being.					
Estimated Budget:	**35 500**										
Funded:											
Unfunded:											
Establishing 2 family child-care centers in pilot villages, 1 family child-care center and opening 1 preschool class in primary school in selected villages	1) At least 90 children of early age benefit from utilizing 3 community-based family child-care centers 2) At least 40 children at the age of 5-6 are better prepared to entering primary school						19 500			Local and district administrations and the communities	Project Officer and District Administration

Conducting a 3-day ECD trainings for 57 preschool workers who do not have preschool educational background in districts	1) 57 preschool workers have improved their knowledge on ECD and learnt how to address children's and families' needs 2) 57 preschool workers have been certified to work with children and families on the legal ground in accordance with ECD policy documents						15 000			UN, NGOs, MoE, University	Project Officer, NGO and University staff
Conducting a three-day ECD Resource Pack Training for government officials	At least 30 government officials have raised their awareness regarding critical ECD issues and enhanced their knowledge on ECD						1 000			UN, other donors	Project Officers/do-norreps

SUB: PROJECT DESCRIPTION: **Policy Development/Advocacy**						OBJECTIVES: - National policies and strategies on ECD are broadly advocated.					
Estimated Budget:	**4 000**										
Funded:											
Unfunded:											
Development of Guidance on Early Learning and Development based on the child's development indicators presented in the State Standard on preschool education and care for a child	Parents/caregivers and specialists (preschool, medical) are able to measure the progress of a child and assess the child's readiness for schooling based on the Guidance on Early Learning and Development						2 000			UN, MoE, ECD thematic group	Project Officers

Reforming the Standard Programme on Education and Development of Children from 1 to 6 years old	Preschool workers improve capacities, efficiency and effectiveness of preschool services based on the Standard Programme on Education and Development of Children from 1 to 6 years old.						2 000			UN, MoE, NGO, experts	Project Officers

Annexe 2

Memorandum of Understanding (MoU) Model

- Draft -

Memorandum of Understanding

Dated...............................

Between

Donor

(In this MoU represented by Programme Manager)

and

Organization

(In this MoU represented by Executive Director

Regarding

Cooperation and Mutual Support
between the "project"
and the implementing organization (NGO) in 'X' country

The partners to this Memorandum of Understanding hereby agree on the following:

1. Goal and Objective of the MoU

(1) The partners to this MoU recognize the importance of working together in the field of HIV prevention, in order to achieve greater synergy and increase their contribution to averting a large-scale HIV/AIDS epidemic, and to decrease the susceptibility of youth and other vulnerable subpopulations (among them sex workers, migrant populations, prisoners, the military and injecting drug users) to HIV.

(2) The objective of this MoU is to outline a partnership of cooperation between the donor and NGO on this specific project.

2. Scope and Fields of Cooperation

(1) While both the donor and NGO will pursue their objectives and work under their respective overarching mandates, the two organizations endeavour to work together in the field of HIV prevention, in order to leverage their individual resources and capacities for a greater contribution to curbing the HIV/AIDS epidemic (in country) than if they operated independently. The cooperation between the partners, and all activities of the partners in the field of HIV prevention, will contribute to the implementation of the State Programme on HIV/AIDS Prevention.

(2) Fields of cooperation between the organizations will include, but not be limited to;

- Sharing resources (national and district offices and facilities, equipment and human resources);
- Jointly developing, and continuously expanding a network of partner organizations active in the fight against HIV/AIDS;
- Conducting joint activities in the areas of training and organizational capacity building;
- Cooperating in the development of messages and materials for behaviour change communication targeting the above-mentioned vulnerable groups;
- Joint use of the existing outreach network of NGO and of the distribution network to be established within the project in order to enhance access to, and coverage of, the target populations for both organizations.

3. Outlook

(1) Due to external restrictions, donor and the NGO will initially remain separate institutions.

For	For
DONOR	NGO
PLACE/COUNTRY...............	PLACE/COUNTRY......
____________________	____________________
Programme Manager	Executive Director

Annexe 3

Business Plan Model for an Organization

A Business Plan

1. Should look at and contain the following key points:
   - Objectives: includes mission, vision statements, area of interest
   - Resources: identifying, using and managing
   - Target audience: understanding needs, strategy, action plans
   - Finances; forecasting, planning, management of funds
   - Activities: key steps, time schedules
2. Aims and Objectives

Aim: (purpose) Objectives: (specific...direct and/or overall) Indicators: (monitoring...measuring impact, performance... evaluations) Achievable and Realistic: (your best estimate...log frame can support for verification/proof) Time Frame: (overall duration of project...or specific project activities)

3. Resources

	Existing Resources	Needed Resources	Strengths
Physical resources			
Professional resources			
Financial resources			

4. Target Audience/Group
   - Situation description (need, statistics, problem statement)
   - Description of target audience (age, condition, environment)
   - Geographic, demographic or economic description

5. Needs assessment/surveys

	Know	Unknown (yet to know)
Information on the target group...age, needs		
Size ...Number of beneficiaries in the project area...% of population		
Factors that influence the target group...priority of their needs, attitudes		
Needed inputs:... equipment, funds, material		
Other players: who is working in the area, donors, government plans		
Opportunities and threats		

6. Needs assessment analysis

Political issues affecting target group	Legislation passed/pending, standards, codes, status of group in community
Economic issues affecting target group	Ability to provide support in kind/cash, migration to other areas... disadvantaged
Sociological issues affecting target group	Attitudes, conflicts, cultural dominance, informal community structures taboos

Technology issues affecting target group	Available technical skills (carpentry, agricultural), running water, electricity

7. Target Group needs and Opportunities

Performance needs	What does your organization need to do…what do you expect in return
Financial needs	What your organization can provide…what is expected from community….other donors
Image needs	How do you present yourself…. are you designing a model community project…

8. Opportunities and Threats

Opportunities	Threats
…donors interested/funding available….niche area for your group….no other groups working in the area…..potential for success because of your approach	…..people too poor to help….no interest from community side…no long term interest from donors…too expensive to implement….no chance of sustainability….

9. Strategy

List proposed activity/service	Description of the activity/service	How and why it's important to beneficiary
Strategies/policies	What you propose and how you plan to enforce the policies	What the beneficiary understands/appreciates about the policies
Location	Accessibility, regularity and continued nature of the activity and service	Is there access all year round... can everyone avail themselves to the services

Communication	How will you promote the activity (media method), create the awareness, get your messages across	How do the beneficiaries receive this information, start process of behavioural change, develop trust

10. Financial Forecasts
    - Projected donor support
    - Activity cost, including administrative recovery
    - Cost efficiencies, proposed, improved operating systems
    - Revenues generated, applied for sustainability.

Annexe 4

Terms of Reference (ToR) Model for a Company

Terms of Reference for Consulting Company Name Here

A. Overview:

In general, Consulting Company will work primarily with the NGO, but will make their services available to all components of the programme as required/requested. The Company will provide services that will primarily focus on social research (qualitative and quantitative) and human resource/management training as it relates to HIV/AIDS prevention and to the capacity and institutional building of the NGO and partners. The Company will provide researchers and trainers of the highest professional quality, who are experienced in research/training, who are able to travel countrywide and who can work independently. The Company will be responsible for the actions and quality of the services they provide and will report directly to the NGO Director, or the concerned officials, as directed. The NGO will prepare a brief research/ training design for each activity that the Company will be assigned. Some activities, as requested/required by the MoH, may have to be advertised/competitively bid. It is the responsibility of the Company to review/revise this design, identify the implementation steps, provide CVs for consideration and approval of the NGO and submit a costing for the assigned activity. The estimated costs and consultants undertaking the activity must be approved by the NGO before the activity begins. A service contract will be issued to the Company for each activity assigned/requested. The Company will be responsible for the finished report/analysis, which must be approved by the NGO before payment is made.

B. Specific Tasks:

Coordinate and work with the NGO in the areas of social research and training for capacity/institutional building.

Advise the NGO Director/staff on the types of research and training that will be appropriate for the NGO to achieve its goals.

- Participate as a partner in the overall AIDS prevention activities, as requested and where the expertise of the Company is useful, for the successful implementation of the entire project.
- Provide inputs for improving the research and training designs, as prepared by the NGO, before implementing the activity.
- Before starting any activity confer/consult with the NGO and seek approval of the NGO Director, and at every stage of implementation keep the NGO Director informed of progress and any problems.

Research

- Before undertaking any research activity the Company must consult along with the NGO Director, with the ministry for approvals and ideas. Also ensure that the activity is not a duplication of other Ministry/NGO or donor ongoing or planned research.
- All research must be undertaken in a culturally sensitive manner, and held in the up most confidence, especially when personal matters are involved.
- Research designs must be approved by the NGO/Ministry, including questionnaire design.
- Reports/findings will be prepared in both English and local language and in the number of copies as requested in the service contract.

Training:

- The same approvals, design requests and implementation steps applied to the research activity (above) also applies to the training/human resource development activities.
- The Company will insure that training courses/modules are prepared/given in the appropriate language of the intended audience
- The Company will ensure that a variety of modern training techniques will be used in the training courses and that evaluation of each training session will be evaluated by the trainees. The evaluation will be given to the NGO Director.
- Specific focus of the training will be to make better programme Managers and lead towards the development and strengthening of local capacity for planning/implementing a programme that assists the Ministry in their national plans for HIV/AIDS prevention.

The Company's tasks include:

<u>Training/human resource development</u>

- Build on/expand the initial marketing and distribution networks to new markets (geographical) pricing policies and product line.
- Capacity development in overall management and staff skills strengthening the NGO as it grows and takes on additional responsibilities.
- Management training in operational and organizational skills in operating an NGO and as the two groups merge their activities.
- Training in monitoring and evaluation techniques/systems, including the development of an MIS.
- Continued training in programme planning.

<u>Studies and research activities</u>

- Consumer and household studies (determine buying habits of condoms/contraceptives, how they receive information about HIV, condom availability etc.) which should follow the branding exercise.

- An evaluation of product acceptance amongst the target group, including impact of IEC/BCC messages.
- Assessment of marketing and sales framework (comparative study on the use of sales team versus use of distributors, length of time a sales person takes at each outlet, project vehicle use versus local transport in making sales calls).

Annexe 5

Terms of Reference (ToR) Model for Individual Consultant

Country Name

Ministry of ?????

Terms of Reference

...... Programme Name

Grant No.

Specialist Needs (finance, management or ?)

For which programme

I Background

The main objective of the programme would be to support the implementation of the first phase of Country's National Strategy during 2004-2015. The support will focus on improving the quality of learning outcomes in all levels of education, expansion of coverage, and the first stage of the reform programme.

The grant provided by the Government of ... Finances activities related to assessment of the needs in developing the quality of ... at all levels of , including but not limited to preparation of a plan for professional development reform; preparation of a framework for evaluation of outcomes; assessment of the technical and professional development needs in management and leadership; setting up implementation arrangements and preparation of Implementation Plan.

Within this framework, the Ministry is going to hire a Consultant/Specialist who will be responsible for financial management issues related to the preparation of the programme activities. The Consultant/Specialist would be working for the Ministry with the Grant Management Expert and with the affiliate institutions of the Ministry with direct reporting to the Grant Manager in the Ministry. Furthermore, the Consultant/Specialist would assist the overall programme preparation process in the Ministry.

II Purpose of this assignment

The main purpose of this assignment is to assist the Ministry in preparing and facilitating the necessary management capacity building to improve the efficient use of resources in this sector. The work should build on progress already made in general in developing financial management systems and procedures in Country name including budgeting, accounting, reporting, internal control and internal audit. This will be based on an institutional and functional analysis of existing financial management capacities of the Ministry, other national education agencies (curriculum, assessment, training and accreditation), municipalities, regional councils, regional and district education departments. The assignment will involve designing organizational development and capacity building activities related to financial management during 2006-2012, including the smooth implementation of a sector-wide approach.

III Scope of the responsibilities

The Consultant/Specialist will be responsible for providing technical assistance and policy advice to the Ministry and to the affiliate institutions including partners/institutions: (i) in the design and implementation of the capacity building activities to strengthen management capacities, and (ii) the preparation of the Financial Management sections as related to the Annual Work Programme 2007. S/he would perform the duties with the highest professional standards and ethics. In particular, the Consultant/Specialist would be responsible for the following tasks:

- Carry out detailed analysis of the existing partners/organizations' procedures and capacities, including strengths and weaknesses on management, including staff capacities of the Ministry affiliate institutions involved in programme implementation;
- Recommend measures for making the management system more reliable, transparent, economic and efficient in support of the overall sector objectives. This would include designing a programme for the sector to enhance transparency of the financial management process; to put in place anti-corruption and corruption reporting measures. For this purpose, collaborate with other agencies dealing with anti-corruption measures;
- Develop an implementation plan for organizational development and capacity building, including different levels of management training programmes, their contents, and outline of training materials to be used, in financial management for 2006-2012 with specific annual development targets and progress indicators;
- Contribute to the preparation of project documents, studies and materials required for the preparation of the programme by the Ministry including the Operation Manual;
- Provide on-the-job training in the tasks listed above to the Ministry staff of the relevant sections in collaboration with the national Management Expert in accordance with the training programmes.

The Consultant/Specialist will work in close cooperation with other consultants hired for programme preparation and coordinate her/his work with the Grant Financial Management Expert.

IV Expected outputs

1. Programme Management Development Plan during 2006-2012;
2. Relevant input to the Operational Manual including Terms of References for all Financial Management Specialists;
3. Management Capacity Building Plan during 2006-2012;

V Reporting requirements

The Consultant/Specialist will report to the Grant Manager (jointly with the local Financial Management Specialist hired under this grant). S/he will also maintain continuous informal reporting to the Ministry on the progress of this assignment. In particular, the Consultant/Specialist will provide:

- Detailed Work Plan no later than 5 working days after signing of the contract,
- Interim Report of all ongoing activities and progress made by May 31,
- Final Report that includes all duties and deliverables mentioned in Section III;

VI Duration of this assignment

This assignment should not exceed 30 (thirty) working days and must be completed by July 31.

VII Qualification Requirements

I General Qualifications

- Minimum University Diploma in management, finance or related field;
- Minimum of 10 years of professional experience in management and financial management preferably with the public sector;

- Certified accountant or similar.

II Specific Qualifications and Professional Experience

- Knowledge of Government administrative, accounting and financial management procedures;
- Knowledge of EU requirements and familiarity with EU directives in the area of public finance management is preferred.

III Other Relevant Experience

- Good report writing skills (samples of the reports prepared by the Consultant on other assignments may be requested for references);
- Good English language skills
- Working level of computer skills, knowledge of MS Office applications, in particular Excel and MS Project.

Annexe 6

Staffing or Manning Chart Model

NAME	FIRM	POSITION	1st	2nd	3rd	4th	5th	6th	7th
INTER-NATIONAL:									
		Team Leader/Social Sector Reform Specialist (3)							
		Child Health Specialist (3)							
		Maternal and Child Nutrition Specialist (2)							

		Early Childhood Education Specialist (3)																												
		Economist/Financial Analyst (1)																												
		SUB-TOTAL 12 P.M.																												
NATIONAL																														
		Social Scientist (4)																												
		Child Health Specialist (6)																												
		Maternal and Child Nutrition Specialist (6)																												

		Early Childhood Education Specialist (6)																												
		Economist/Financial Analyst (4)																												
To be selected		Oblast Coordinators (10)																												
		SUB-TOTAL 36 pm																												

Annexe 7

Organization Capability Statement Model (can be included in technical proposals and visibility materials)

Capability Statement

Company 'X' and associates, is an American-Romanian commercial firm engaged in training, social research, social marketing and programme management.

Company 'X' and associates is a legally registered SRL in Romania with its headquarters in Bucharest and a branch office in the USA. Company was established to assist emerging nations and developing countries build local capacities through improved human resource development and modern training techniques. The Company's offices are fully equipped with computers, printers and photo copy machine and connected by e-mail and phone/fax for easy interface. Please visit our web site for additional information.

- Company was established in 1999, and has undertaken assignments in eleven (11) different countries, including Moldova, Albania, Romania, Lebanon, Yemen, Ethiopia, Namibia, Kenya, Mali, Kyrgyzstan and Indonesia. Company's clients include The World Bank, KfW, UNICEF, UNDP, USAID and the private sector. Several of the Company assignments have been for the same client, and in the same country, but on different technical assistance activities. In addition to direct TA, many training courses are provided by the Company staff to institutions like Liverpool School of Tropical Medicine, among others. Work references are available from clients in Romania and from the international organizations mentioned above. Bank accounts have been established at the Commercial Bank.

- The Company maintains a core staff of 4 professionals – sociologists, trainers and social marketing specialists - who are supported by two administrators for legal and financial support. The core staff is a mixture of Romanian and American professionals. Language capabilities within the Company for translating or training materials development, include Romanian, English, French and Bahasa, Indonesian, German and Hindi. Language skills are available through the Company associates. The Company has also associated with local Romanian NGOs and consultants in the field of human resource development.
- The owners of the Company are working partners in the firm's programme activities and together have over 50 years of hands-on experience. Because the Company staff have lived and worked in Europe's emerging nations and Africa's developing countries we bring both a wide range of technical expertise plus the actual field experience necessary to design good management systems and training courses, including training of trainers' programmes.
- The Company prides itself for being focused and practical in its approach. The research activities, both qualitative and quantitative, always develop and then pre-test, any questionnaire before undertaking the survey. Likewise, training needs assessments are undertaken before designing any training course in an effort to meet the participant's needs. The needs assessment is free of charge to the client. The Company's training is pro-active and includes a complete range of organization and programme management skills, plus social marketing. A list of training materials is available on request.
- In addition to training, the Company has demonstrated its capability in undertaking both long and short term

assignments in the technical field of integrated rural development, reproductive health, including HIV/AIDS prevention, health reform campaigns, sanitation, rural water supply and contraceptive and commodity procurement. The Company has worked with both local and international development partners in this wide range of development activities in Eastern Europe, Central Asia, Africa and Southeast Asia. Specific project profiles, detailing the training or consulting activity, is available upon request.

Project Experience Relevant to Vietnam

PROJECT	COUNTRY	YEAR
1. Oral Contraceptive Study	Vietnam (KfW)	1996
2. HIV/AIDS Project Design	PDR Laos (UNICEF)	1997/98
3. Condom Procurement/ CSM	Albania (KfW)	ongoing
4. Condom Procurement/CSM	Namibia (KfW)	1999-2001
5. Condom Procurement/CSM	China (UNFPA)	ongoing
6. Condom Procurement/CSM	Uganda (KfW)	1997-99

CSM = Condom Social Marketing

In addition, the Company experience extends into all aspects of HIV/AIDS prevention including programme appraisal and design, development of IE&C and BCC materials and programme implementation. The Company has worked in programmes similar to the needs of the Vietnam programme in 11 different countries, including 5 countries in South and South East Asia.

Annexe 8

Log Frame Model

Logical Framework Analysis: Detailed Output Summary and Implementation Plan

INTERVENTION LOGIC (Objectives and Narrative Summary)	VARIABLE INDICA-TORS	MEANS OF VERIFIC-ATION	ASSUMP-TIONS/ COMMENTS
The overall objective of the project is to build the capacity of the Administrative Reform and Civil Service Commission to design and support the implementation of interim reforms in key ministries and departments and evaluate the impact of this work on an ongoing basis.	New and improved key functions for commis-sion; Better linkages between commission and different Ministries and governmental agencies; Improved personnel management system.	Programme components interim reports and final report; New working methodo-logies, reports, strategy documents and manuals; Training and study tours reports; Commission Training and Resource Center.	It is assumed that the project will have positive political environment; It is assumed that the election process to take place in mid 2010 will not create major administrative blockage;
PROJECT PURPOSE The general purpose of the technical assistance is to build the capacity of commission, to help partners to establish a	New merit-based appoint-ments, promotion	Needs assessment and research; Working methodo-	It is assumed that existing documents and statistics are available for the project;

capacity and improve performance in key ministries and departments through the development and implementation of merit based appointment and promotion procedures, improved public service management and provide support to line ministries to prepare administrative reform programme.	and appeals procedures for senior civil service posts and for the remainder of the Civil Service; New Civil Service law amend-ments of the existing legislation on Civil Service Employ-ment, new personnel policies and new procedures for implementi-ng the civil laws; Commission capacitate in order to facilitate the develop-ment of proposals for restructuring ministries	logies and implementation plans; Training sessions; HR data base; Training and Resource Center within Commission; Project reports delivered in time and approved by the Client and its Working Group; Interim and final reports approved.	It is assumed that relevant document will be translated without delay from English to local language and vice versa; It is assumed that the project will be implemented without delays to insure effective project implemen-tation; Various stakeholders will maintain interest for the project and will not change their structure.

	and departments under the reform decree.		
OBJECTIVE 1. To build the capacity of Commission and the Civil Service Commissioners on management of appointments and appeals procedures. Outputs: - Work programme and management procedures for the Independent Recruitment and Appeals Boards are reviewed and analysed;	a) Descriptive reports on review and analysis of legislation and normative arrangements on appointment and appeals and working procedures; work programme and management procedures reviewed and analysed;	a) Reports submitted and approved by the Client and its Working Group;	a) It is assumed that the Client provides relevant statistical and activity reports.

-Training program on good practices in Appointment and Appeals procedures implemented;-Study tours for selected public servants in countries where the Appointment/Recruitment and Appeals system was already reformed;	b) report on training program	b) idem;	b) It is assumed that Commission staff will allocate time to work
- The IT support for HR database containing the names of eligible and suitable qualified candidates for appointments improved;	c) report on improvement of HR data base;	c) idem	c) Report on study tours with the Consultant.
- Methodology for reporting and monitoring the activity of Commission and the Independent Recruitment and Appeals Boards developed and implemented.	d) report on established methodo-logy on reporting and monitoring Commission and Indepen-dent Recruitment and Appeals Boards.	d) idem.	

ACTIVITIES	MEANS	INPUTS
Objective 1. To build the capacity of Commission and Civil Service Commissioners on management of appointments and appeals procedures. Outputs: Reports on: review and analysis and working procedures on appointment and appeals. Work programme and management procedures for the Independent Recruitment and Appeals Boards. Methodology on reporting and monitoring procedures for Commission and Independent Recruitment and Appeals Boards. Improved IT system for HR data base; Training programme Study tour programme	Analysis of secondary statistical data, collection and analysis of primary data, legislation analysis, analysis of descriptive documents, in-depth interviews of key staff and Commissioners; HR data base IT system improved; Training; Study tours (2); Working procedures documents.	International TA: Local TA:

HIV/AIDS Prevention Programme, Kyrgyzstan	Logical Framework	Country: Kyrgyzstan Duration: 2005/08	Prepared by : Jim Myers
Descriptive Summary	Verifiable Indicators	Means of Verification	Assumptions
Goal			
Reduce the spread of HIV/AIDS epidemic in Kyrgyzstan	Prevalence of HIV among target group remains below X %	Sentinel surveillance results	Political situation remains stable Other AIDS prevention components implemented
Programme purpose			
Improvement of the national HIV/AIDS prevention strategy	Reliable estimates for target group exist	Statistics department of National AIDS center	Improved knowledge of the epidemiological situation
Outputs			
HIV surveillance established according to UNAIDS guidelines	Effective second generation surveillance system established	External evaluation and programme reports	Successful coordination with other AIDS prevention organizations

VCT available to target group	Number of VCT centers established	Programme and counselling reports	Government supports the setting up of VCT centers

NOTE: These are two samples of a Log Frame...there are several different variations. The required design often depends on the donor's demands/format. Include whatever information/format it takes to give the donor a 'logical' picture of what you hope to achieve and how you will monitor and measure the results.

Annexe 9

Monitoring and Evaluation Plan

A monitoring and evaluation plan should be included in each project document and monitoring activities should be scheduled in the annual implementation work plan.

Objec-tives	Activity	Indicators	Data Source	Methods	Person Responsible	Time Frame

NOTE: Please remember 'monitoring' tracks progress and 'evaluation' seeks answers!

Annexe 10

Organization Model

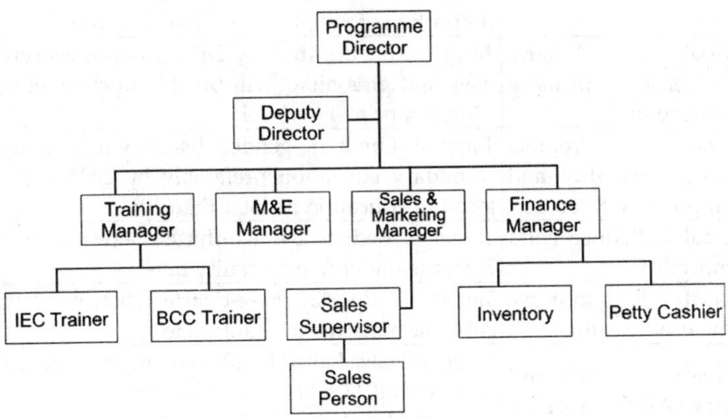

Annexe 11

Millennium Development Goals

Goals	Targets
Goal 1: Eradicate extreme poverty and hunger	Target 1: Halve, between 1990 and 2015, the proportion of people whose income is less than one dollar a day (PPP). Target 2: Halve, between 1990 and 2015, the proportion of people who suffer from hunger.
Goal 2: Achieve universal primary education	Target 3: Ensure that, by 2015 children everywhere, boys and girls alike, will be able to complete a full course of primary school.
Goal 3: Promote gender equality and empower women	Target 4: Eliminate gender disparity in primary and secondary education preferably by 2005 and to all levels of education no later than 2015
Goal 4: Reduce child mortality	Target 5: Reduce by two-thirds, between 1990 and 2015, the under five mortality rate.
Goal 5: Improve maternal health	Target 6: Reduce by three-quarters, between 1990 and 2015, the maternal mortality rate.
Goal 6: Control HIV/AIDS, malaria and other diseases	Target 7: Halve halted by 2015 and begun to reverse the spread of HIV/AIDS. Target 8: Have halted by 2015 and begun to reverse the incidence of malaria and other major diseases.
Goal 7: Ensure environmental sustainability	Target 9: Integrate the Principles of sustainable development into country policies and programmes and reverse the loss of environmental resources. Target 10: Halve, by 2015, the proportion of people without sustainable access to safe drinking water Target 11: By 2020, to have achieved a significant improvement in the lives of at least 100 million slum dwellers.
Goal 8: Develop a global partnership for development	Target 12: Develop further an open, rule-based, predictable, non-discriminatory trading and financial system. Includes a commitment to good governance, development, and poverty reduction – both nationally and internationally

Index

M

N

O

P

R

S

T

V

W